# My Father's Mansion

## by George Elliott Windish

ISBN-10: 1480172537

EAN-13: 9781480172531

Library of Congress Control Number: 2012920556

CreateSpace Independent Publishing Platform

North Charleston, South Carolina

# About the Cover

In the 1940's and 1950's the electric company in Western Maryland, Potomac Edison System, sent out inserts with their electric bills every other month that had a picture of places of interest on its cover as well as a two month calendar. The insert also included safety tips and warnings about electricity, an explanation of the place of interest picture and Blue Ribbon recipes relative to the season.

In June of 2008 a dear high school friend of mine, Alice Zehrbach, found one of Potomac Edison's inserts, the one with Windale on it, in her mother's things and sent it to me with the following note "I'm so happy I found this for you; bittersweet memories. A beautiful house because it was a home full of love". I want to thank you Alice for your friendship and for providing the cover for "My Fathers Mansion".

# Dedication

*I dedicate this book to my daughter Holly.*
*I present this window in time, this slice of my heart*
*that we could not share otherwise.*
*This is my way to thank her for all the love and*
*joy she has brought into my life.*

# Prologue

Each of us moves through many passages in our lifetime. Some are more memorable than others; some are good, and some are not so good. Each of those passages can be broken down into expectations, experiences, and events that define the passage itself. Going one step further, each passage or chapter of our lives becomes part of us and defines what we've become and why.

It isn't often that we clearly understand ourselves and how we became what we are. So I decided to put into writing a time or passage in my life that I call my formative years, those years being between six and eighteen years of age. These years were a time of innocence, trust, and discovery for me, a time when I found myself and a profound love for all of God's creations, a time when the world opened up to me and invited me in.

What I set out to do was enable my wife, Linda, and my daughter, Holly, (and even myself) to better understand just why I am the person they know today, to give them and myself insight into the complexities I'm sure I present from time to time.

Secondarily, I wanted to tell the world of a time when life was profoundly different from what it is today. My wish is that this book will provide a record of life back in the late forties and fifties, as well as the story of my growing up. It was a time of transition and one of great hope, a simpler time, but still complex. For me, this time is crystal clear and written from my heart. A story I want to share with all who read it.

# Chapter 1

# Windale

Windale Farms was the name of the farm I grew up on; well, not entirely, I was six years of age when I moved there in 1945. Windale was the name my father and mother came up with when they purchased the farm in 1943, which, when I think about it, was a pretty good name. It's a derivative of our family name *Windish*, which is Austrian and used to be spelled Windisch, and the noun *dale*, which means a small valley or a place between two hills, and it fit very well because that's exactly where it was located and exactly who lived there. I don't know if that's what Mom and Dad thought, but it was a great choice. Windale was located about seven miles north of Cumberland, Maryland, on Union Grove Road, or Mason Road, depending on who you talked to; there were no signs back then, and the farm was about two miles south of the Mason Dixon Line in the Evitt's Creek Valley. The Evitt's Creek Valley runs north and south between Evitt's Mountain to the east and Will's Mountain to the west. Windale was located on a small bluff just above the floodplain of Evitt's Creek. If you look on a map, you can easily find its location. Maryland is less than ten miles wide between Cumberland, which is located on the Potomac River across from Ridgeley, West Virginia, and the Pennsylvania state line (or Mason Dixon Line). If you find Route 220 or Bedford Valley Road, sometimes called the Bedford Pike just north of Cumberland, you are probably within a mile or so of the house.

As I said earlier, I was only six years old when I moved to Windale. Before that, my family had lived in LaVale, Maryland, which is located west of Cumberland on the west side of Will's Mountain on Route 40, also known as the National Pike. My father purchased the farm from Doc and Daisy Wilson, who were descendants of the Smouse family that originally built it. The purchase consisted of 250 acres and the house that stood on it and was finalized in 1943. The old home was in a bad state of disrepair, as most of the house had not been lived in for a long time. There was no running water or electricity in the old place. The Wilsons used oil lamps and had a hand pump to bring in water from a spring not too far from the house. They only used three rooms

*Windale before remodeling*

of the house: the kitchen, which contained the hand pump for water and a stove for cooking and heat; a room off the kitchen to the west, which was most likely used for sleeping; and the old dining room to the north, which contained the door onto the back porch. Because of my age at that time, I am relying on word-of-mouth information that came to me from my family and friends for some of this information. I'm quite sure, though, that for the most part the information is correct.

With that understanding, I would like to tell you a little more about the homestead. The house my dad purchased was not the original; that original house, built by Henry Smouse, probably in the 1790s, was constructed of wood and burned down. Built by John Jacob Smouse, Henry's son, the present-day home was built on the site of the original and completed in 1845. Henry Smouse (Schmouse), who emigrated from Germany, was given a grant of about six hundred acres from the governor of Maryland, William Paca, a signer of the Declaration of Independence, as a reward for his participation in the Revolutionary War. The Smouse homestead consisted of a large gristmill and a mill-race (which had its head on Evitt's Creek about a mile or so north of the mill), barns, chicken houses, a wagon shed, a number of tenant houses, a blacksmith shop, a hay shed, a mule barn, and corn cribs.

When my father purchased the farm, it consisted of the house built in 1845, two tenant houses, a chicken coop, a hay barn, and some out-buildings attached to the back of the main house. They had been used as a dining room, a summer kitchen, an icehouse, a blacksmith shop, and a wood storage area. I think it would be safe to say the icehouse, blacksmith shop, and wood storage area may have had other uses over the century that the house stood, but that's all lost to history. As near as I can account, all those who could have verified their purpose have departed this world. I do know, however, that my father tore down the last three of the outbuildings and salvaged the first two, which were the old dining room and kitchen. He converted them into the back foyer and laundry room of the present-day house. Where the last three stood, he built a three-car garage with an apartment upstairs for his in-laws to live if they pleased.

The house was about one hundred years old then, and given the state of its condition, my father was taking on a Herculean task. The house was rapidly returning to Mother Nature. I wasn't there yet, but I heard all the stories about snakes in the walls as well as their lounging in fireplaces. Field vermin nests were everywhere, bats were in the attic among other places, and many chimney swifts were in almost every flue, of which there were six, all two stories high. Of course, insects of all nature and kind had taken over everywhere. But I don't think that bothered my father any: he understood the history of the old house; he had a vision of what this old relic could become; he had a dream that he could restore it to its original glory, give it a new life, and introduce it to another century.

The renovation took about two years, which was aggravated by the lack of materials needed due to the Second World War. The house was a two-story Southern plantation–style home. There was a large front porch with four large columns that supported the upstairs porch, which was covered with a beautiful portico. Each room of the house was constructed on its own foundation, of which there were eight on the first floor. For the most part, the second floor was a duplication of the first floor, which added up to sixteen rooms in the main house. The walls were made of locally fired red brick and were two bricks thick with an air space between the two layers to provide for insulation in both summer and winter. I know this for a fact from the times I had to crawl around under the house for various reasons, which I will expound on in later stories. I learned at an early age the true meaning of "crawl space." Also, just hold on to those questions about how I got through all those foundations.

The roof was constructed of oak with tin roofing covering it. The wood, no doubt, was cut on the property, and I think one could safely say all the wood in the house was cut there. There were eleven windows on the front of the house (or south side), four to the east, seven to the north, and none on the west side for a total of twenty-two. I suspect the windows were still the original ones; they were single-pane wood frames with the glass puttied in. The glass was distorted, some with bubbles, no doubt from the manufacturing process and its age; I was told one time that glass actually runs over time and distorts itself.

There was a total of five exterior doors in the main house: a large front door leading into the downstairs foyer that opened onto the front porch and a smaller door that opened off the back of the foyer to the back of the house, another door in the upstairs foyer that opened onto the upstairs porch, still another door that opened onto the back porch, and one last door that opened to the outside from the most southeastern first-floor room, which dad replaced with a window when he remodeled, for a total of five.

The old house had six functional fireplaces and two woodstoves. This should give you a pretty good visual picture of what Dad had to work with, keeping in mind that it was in a bad state of disrepair.

The first thing he did was to remove all the windows and doors and had them sent to the mill to be repaired and restored. His objective was to restore as much of the old house that he could to its original state. Next, he had what was left of the plaster removed. Plaster back then, in the days the house was built, was made with horsehair and applied to the lathing that supported it. I remember my father telling the story about the excessive amount of dust created when the plaster and lathing were removed. Someone driving by on Union Grove Road, which was about one hundred yards from the house (keep in mind the windows had all been removed), called the fire company thinking the house was on fire. As you can imagine, there was a lot of plaster and lathing that came from those sixteen rooms, and it was all thrown out the back windows of the house into one huge pile. Due to the shortage of gasoline because of the war, Dad decided that, rather than have it hauled away, he would flatten it out the best he could, build a brick wall around it, cover it with a good portion of dirt, and plant grass, which converted a pile of trash into a beautiful and functional patio that we would enjoy in later years.

The next step of the restoration was to install all the electrical and plumbing for the whole house. Since all the plaster walls and ceilings were removed, the electrical wiring installation was made much simpler. However, since the house was to be heated by hot water, there was a great deal more plumbing to do than just for the palatable water system.

The spring I mentioned earlier that the Wilsons used would become the water source for the house. Located within fifty feet of the house, it had a great flow rate, with clear, sweet water. By the way, it is still in use today. I should explain that it was a sister spring to two others that were also quite close to the house. One of them was a free-flowing spring located about 150 feet to the north that eventually emptied into Evitt's Creek. It never dried up, and I used it to root Weeping Willow sprouts, which I planted all over the farm. The other was found at about the same distance to the east of the house; however, this spring, its temperature around fifty-five degrees, was used to cool fresh milk and was covered with a walk-in springhouse that could be closed to the outside. I should mention that all three of these springs flowed from a shale bank that was about fifty feet from the house; it ran along where the old millrace used to be, then curved to the east. My father had a brick Quonset hut–type springhouse built into the shale bank over the spring that would supply water to the house and an overflow pipe that went to the small run the spring to the north created. I mention all three springs now because I will refer to them later.

Back to the plumbing! The original builders of the house had dug out a root cellar under the southeast corner of the house, which was about twenty-five by thirty feet in size. That's where Dad installed the pump to bring the spring water to the house. It was a good choice too, since that's where he planned to install the furnace for the house's heating system. No matter how cold it got, he wouldn't have to worry about the pump or the pressure tank or its plumbing freezing up.

Remember those six fireplaces I mentioned? They all had to be re-built. The firebrick was burned out, the flues had to be replaced, each hearth and mantelpiece had to be rebuilt, and each of the six chimneys had to be pointed. When the house was finished, I had one of those fireplaces in my bedroom.

The last major project was refinishing the floors, which had been subjected to water damage from a roof leak as well as many years of mopping and wear. Luckily, the flooring consisted mostly of termite resistant heart of pine, although I suspect some of the floors also were made from hemlock, of which there was a sizable grove on a bluff just above the millrace head north of the house. Some of the boards had to be replaced, but most were salvageable even though they were cupped and uneven. Dad decided to sand them down as they lay. Old floors like this differ from floors of today, as the boards were custom laid in multiple lengths and widths. The floorboards were about one and half inches thick, so there was plenty of wood to smooth down the edges and make the floor smooth, and it really turned out beautiful. I love old wood that is restored, and even as a child, I admired those floors.

It's strange that I know all of these things, but I intently listened to these stories from my father. Then I would later check them out as to what had been done and why to make sure I understood what I was being told, and now it's as if I were there when it was happening. I became fascinated with the old house and its history, and it very much became part of my life. I felt as though I was a part of it, and it was a part of me. I was so proud and lucky that I lived there. Living in that house taught me how important our ancestors were and what a great legacy they left for us. But I must say that the most important thing I learned while living there—with my mom and dad, my two sisters, and my brother, as well as all four of my grand-parents—was how valuable family is to learning how you should live your life and how to deal with whatever life throws at you along the way.

*Windale renovated*

# Chapter 2

# Albert Elliott Windish

My father was born on July 8, 1902, to George and Vernona (Elliott) Windish in Camden, New Jersey. I know very little about his childhood; he never talked about it to me, nor did his mother and father. I think that's unusual, but that's how it was. I do know that he only completed seven grades in school, so I suspect that he was mostly self-taught. He was an avid reader, and in his spare time, there was always a book in his hand. He developed a library of his own during the course of his lifetime, of which I still have some of the books today.

I also know that, as a young man in the later part of the 1920s, he and another fellow took a cross-country trip to California in an automobile one summer. Again, he never talked about it, but I discovered some pictures that were taken on the trip. It was fascinating to me that he had done it, and I knew I would do it myself someday. I know that, also as a young man, he drove a team of mules at a clay pit located somewhere near Philadelphia.

I know that he and my mother married and started a family later than most. Dad eventually got into the grocery business and worked for American Stores grocery chain. He then moved to Johnstown, Pennsylvania, with that company and had a route servicing stores in the western areas of Pennsylvania and Maryland. His route included Cumberland, Maryland. Shortly thereafter, he decided he wanted to live in Cumberland and start his own business. So he moved my mother and sister, Christina, to LaVale, Maryland, just outside of Cumberland to the west. In 1939, the same year I was born, he opened a store called Stacey's Market, which was named after my mother's maiden name. The market was located at 51 North Center Street in downtown Cumberland in a building that would eventually succumb to urban renewal.

Besides dry goods, Dad specialized in seafood, mainly from the Chesapeake Bay, as well as local fresh fruit and vegetables. His business was very successful, and Stacey's became well known right away for its high quality and good service. It wasn't long before he opened another store in Cumberland on Baltimore Avenue and then a road stand on the National Pike between LaVale and Frostburg, Maryland. The National Pike was a toll road at one time, and Dad's road stand was near the old tollhouse, which is still there today just across the road. In later years, he also started a wholesale produce business called Valley Produce, which provided fresh produce to retail stores throughout the tristate area. Dad was a real entrepreneur!

*Albert Windish, my Sister Christina, dog Donnie and horse Sunny*

# Chapter 3

# A New Life

When completed, the main house also consisted of the retained back foyer, which had a washroom and the stairs down to the old root cellar where the furnace and the spring water pump were located. The furnace was actually a low-pressure boiler with two hot-water circulating systems—one system to heat the main house and the other system to heat everything else. It was a coal-fired furnace with an automatic stoker system to feed the coal when called for.

It was my job, as soon as I was old enough, to tend the furnace every day, which I usually did after dinner. The first thing I did was to take out the coal slag, or clinkers, as they were called. The clinkers formed a hard ring around the mouth of the stoker feeder in the center of the firebox. To get them out, I had to take a large heavy bar, about six feet long, and break it up, hopefully into four pieces. Once broken, I took a claw-type tool about the same length that was designed so that, when you turned the handle, one of the claws would open up and you would grip the broken clinker and remove it from the furnace. I piled the red-hot clinkers in front of the furnace and then pulled the remaining burning coal to the center of the firebox with a hoe-type tool. When the stoker ran and brought in new coal, the new coal would catch fire and continue the process.

Once in a while, the system didn't work, and the fire would go out, which was a real problem because the furnace would call for the stoker to bring in coal, which it did until someone shut it off, and the whole firebox would fill up with unburned coal. When that happened, I had to shovel out the unburned coal and then restart the fire, and it was a dirty, dusty job. The coal that had been through the stoker was ground up into a fine powder by the stoker worm and made a lot of dust when moved. It is no wonder that, even today, I have a weak respiratory system after breathing in all that coal dust.

Of course, it didn't help that, around that time, I decided I was going to start smoking. My dad and his mother and father smoked, so I guess I thought it was OK for me to start. They didn't know I smoked, or at least I thought they didn't, so taking care of the furnace every night gave me a great opportunity to have a smoke without anyone knowing it. I would squat down on my haunches in front of the open firebox door and smoke away, all my smoke traveling into the furnace and up the chimney, not up into the house, so I thought my smoking secret was safe. I have often thought if they wondered why it took me so long to tend the furnace.

The other step in regularly tending the furnace was to take out the clinkers each week. It was also a dirty job, as you had to break up the cooled clinkers with a small maul and fill five gallon buckets with them, and then pass the buckets through the coal shoot to someone, usually my sister Christina, who would dump them into a trailer. Later, I could spread them on the driveway. Over the years, it made a great base for the driveway, given that we burned between thirty and thirty-five tons of coal to heat that house every year. The remaining two jobs were only done once a year. The first was emptying the furnace flu, which I really liked to do. When I opened the door to the flu of the chimney, the fly ash ran like water out of it into a ten-gallon oil drum—it was amazing stuff. The second was done in the fall when we first turned on the heating systems. I had to take a radiator key and let out any air that had accumulated in the radiators.

If I needed to get under the main house, I could take up a few of the root cellar steps. There was one such an occasion that I recall very vividly. The water pump from the spring had been running for no apparent reason, and Dad decided that there must be a leak in the heating system pipes under the house. Someone had to go under and check it out. Guess who that someone was? I was volunteered because I was male and the only one in the family small enough to fit under there. I don't know why, but I didn't use a flashlight. I went under with a light bulb at the end of a very long electrical cord. Since I had never been under there before, I really didn't know how to get around. The crawl space under the house was about eighteen inches high, and I was told that there were openings in the foundations that I could get through. They were opened when the house was plumbed for the heating system.

Mother was above the floor tracking my every move. I would tap on the floor, and she would tap back. I followed the heating pipes through one, then two foundations and didn't see any problems. After I had checked out the whole system and found nothing wrong, I was about as far away from the root cellar as I could get, lying on my back talking to Mom through the floor. I told her I couldn't find any leaks and was coming out. I rolled over onto my stomach—and inadvertently, the light bulb. *Pop!* It was gone. God, it was so dark. I don't think I had ever seen darkness like that. For a second, I was really terrified. How could I ever find my way out? Then I remembered the light cord. All I had to do was follow it, which was only about eighty feet. Just then I my thoughts turned to what else could have been under there with me. Spiders! Which I really have a fear of. Snakes! Snakes live under houses; maybe there were snakes under there with me. Being under there without the light was just like being blind. I continued following the cord and finally found my way out. As it turned out, the water leak was the toilet in the apartment. As I look back on what happened, now it seems rather comical, but it sure wasn't then.

Besides the back foyer, which was on the northeast side of the main house, there was the laundry room, which was equipped with a Bendix front-loading washing machine (way ahead of its time), two large washtubs with a large wooded cover that did double duty as a table, and one of those General Electric ironers called a mangle that Mom sat in front of to operate. It had a rotating roller about three feet long with a heated ironing arm, which was the same length as the roller it cradled and could be lowered automatically and lifted from it. The operator would simply run whatever was to be ironed over the roller and close the heating arm on it, turning it through.

At my dad's grocery and seafood store, all the employees wore white aprons that hung on their necks and were tied in the back. Boy, they went through a lot of them every week. Dad always had a two-week supply, so the store never ran out. Each week, the dirty aprons were brought home, and Mom would wash, bleach, and starch them, then hang them outside to dry. Mom then ran the aprons through the GE ironer. She was quite good at it. She was an amazing woman.

The main house had a beautiful large living room with two fire-places. Mom and Dad usually spent their evenings there, Dad reading as he always did and Mother sewing, knitting, doing needlepoint, or just darning socks over an old light bulb. Sometimes, on special oc-casions, both fireplaces were burning. That was always a very memo-rable time. Mother and Dad loved show tunes, and we had a consol record player on which they always played the old 78 or 33 records. I remember songs from "South Pacific," "Oklahoma," "Annie Get Your Gun," and others. I liked to lie on the floor and do my homework and listen to the music. Even today, I know many of the lyrics of those songs from back then. Those are cherished memories for me.

When the house was renovated, Dad built a beautiful solarium on the west wall of the main house. Though quite small, it was one of my favorite places to be. Low bookcases, topped with plants of all kinds, lined the walls beneath the windows. A casual wooden-armed couch and matching chair were the only pieces of furniture. The north, west, and south walls were all glass windows that could roll out if de-sired. When the sun poured into that room in the wintertime, it was just lovely. My grandmother Windish had a green thumb, and I suspect that Dad built the solarium for her. She mainly took care of all the plants, and she grew the most beautiful angel's wing begonias I have ever seen, standing at least six feet tall, always in bloom.

Also in the wintertime, I remember sitting out there in the dark and watching for my father to turn off Bedford Road and onto Union Grove Road on his way home from work. He was usually on time, so I would watch the car that I thought was him come down into the valley, and if it made the turn into the drive, which was quite long, I would run through the house, alerting everyone that he was coming, then into the garage, throwing open the door just as he got there. He never said anything about me doing it, but I know he must have appreciated it. I also used to shine his shoes twice a week, and he never said anything about that, either. Dad was a hard man that way, and it was hard for me to understand and to ever become close to him.

The rest of the main house downstairs consisted of a den with a fireplace. Mainly, that's where Dad did his business calls and Mother would write. Next to the den was the breakfast room, which had a door to a modern kitchen for its day. The den and breakfast rooms were taken over by the television when we got one. For everyone to watch, we had to use both rooms. Off the kitchen was a beautiful formal dining room with a huge picture of Mary at the tomb of Jesus. The room contained a very large dining table—large enough to accommodate the entire family of ten when we were all together. It was used for all meals: breakfast, lunch, and dinner. All rules of etiquette applied. Remember, most times, we had a mother and two grandmothers at that table. We had to sit properly, no elbows on the table, and we had to remain quiet unless we were asked to speak. We had to eat what was on our plate and could only leave the table when excused. Each person at the table had an assigned place to sit.

I was a lousy eater because I didn't like meat, so I got into hot water quite often with Dad. Luckily for me, I sat by my grandfather Windish, whom I called Grandpop. On one particular Sunday morning when we all were having fried eggs, I just couldn't eat one of the two I had on my plate. Noticing that I was in trouble with Dad for not wanting to eat what was in front of me, Grandpop saved the day when

Dad wasn't looking. Suddenly, Grandpop reached over and, in one quick movement, forked the egg, putting the whole thing in his mouth at one time, and it was gone! I can't tell you how many times I have told that story.

One other breach of etiquette that occurred that I must relate is about something my sister Gloria did. One evening, in the wintertime, we were all sitting at the table having dinner. Our cat Porgy jumped up on the windowsill outside and was meowing to come in. He kept it up and kept it up, so finally, Gloria, who sat in front of the window, being six or seven at the time, got up and opened the window for him to come in. When she opened the window, the cat jumped down off the windowsill, not inside but back outside to the yard. Gloria closed the window, turned around, and said, "That son of a bitch." Well, you could have heard a pin drop, to say nothing of the jaws. She sat down, and not a word was said. I guess everyone agreed.

And lastly, upstairs, there was a sewing room, which doubled as a nursery just off the master bedroom, with a full bath off of that. There was also another full bath upstairs that serviced the remaining three bedrooms. The total number of heated rooms in the house was twenty-two, due to the living room using two of the original rooms as well as the two baths upstairs taking another, leaving thirteen of the original sixteen rooms in the main house.

What a wonderful restoration job. It was just magnificent. I may not have noticed at the time, being only six years old, but the older I got, the more I realized just what my father had done. He had a dream, and he made it real for all of us, including his mother and father and my mom's mother and father. Christina and I really felt special. We had our own bedroom with a fireplace, which Christina later shared with Gloria, as I did later with my brother David, who was born a few years after we moved into the house.

My father was a well-respected businessman who provided well for the entire family. As I said before, many nights, there were ten of us around the dinner table, which was a great tribute to his dream. Those were times that are embedded in my memory; times that will always make me a part of his dream.

# Chapter 4

# Getting Started

Windale Farms had not been a working farm for a great many years before we moved there. The farm may have had some of the pasture-land leased out or just provided to other farmers in the area to use, but there wasn't any objective or plan to the farming that was done.

My father liked to ride horses, and both he and my mother each had a horse—one named Bob and the other Sonny—they rode them quite often. Christina and I also had ponies. But I doubt that Dad knew much about farming. My grandfather, on the other hand, had farmed in Jennerstown, Pennsylvania, before he moved to Cumberland to live with us in LaVale, so I'm sure my dad used him as a resource. Anyway, my dad wanted to have a working farm, so he set out to get it up and running. We had two tenant houses, one of which was remodeled so that, when the time came, a tenant farmer could be hired to tend the farm work, someone who knew what it took to run a farm.

I was too young at that time to help with the remodeling, but each time we changed tenant farmers, it was my job to repaint all four rooms. I didn't like to paint and usually made a mess, not on purpose, but because I just wasn't good at painting and didn't want to be. Yet I did what I was told. I remember one time in particular that I was told to paint the tenant house when it was cold, below freezing. So rather than crank up the woodstove, I decided to use a portable charcoal stove that my dad used in his wholesale business delivery trucks to keep vegetables and the like from freezing or to keep the banana room at the warehouse from getting too cold. Anyway, I found out later that this was not such a good idea.

I didn't realize at the time that charcoal burning in an enclosed room fills it with carbon monoxide. The first thing I noticed was that I got this really bad headache and couldn't think right—I guess my painting was really sloppy then. I decided to go outside to get some air and started to feel better, but dummy me; I went back in and started painting again! However, it wasn't long until I really started to feel bad again, so I went up to the house to see Mom. Well, as you suspect, she wasn't too happy with her dumb son after I told her what I was doing. It could have turned out really bad. If I had passed out, no one would have found me in time. When I was out doing things around the farm, no one expected me until mealtimes. A lesson well learned. The next time I painted the tenant house, I lit the woodstove to warm up the house.

The remodeled tenant house was located just down the road southwest of the main house, maybe a hundred yards or so. The house had four rooms with electricity but no running water: a kitchen, living area, and two bedrooms upstairs. The kitchen had a large woodstove for cooking and heating, and a table for eating meals. Also, there was a flue running from the downstairs living area to the upstairs bedroom that was connected to a small wood or coal stove in each of those rooms.

For water, there was a pure, clean spring with a good flow not far from the back porch. The spring flowed from the bottom up and was contained by a large terra-cotta pipe, which held probably twenty to thirty gallons of water. Of course, it had to be fetched and brought to the house for cooking, washing, and bathing. I should mention that there was always a metal dipper at the spring so one could have a refreshing cold drink on a hot summer day.

About three yards to the right of the spring was a root cellar dug into the shale bank—we called it "the cave." The front entrance was concealed with stout timbers and thick boards covered in tar paper, and the rest were underground. It also had a heavy door that could be closed to keep the coolness in during the summer and the cold out during the winter. It is my understanding that ice was cut from Evitt's Creek and stored in the root cellar to assist the cooling in the summer, but not when I lived there. The tenant families used it to store numerous fruits and vegetables that they grew in a large garden just across from the cave and the spring.

I should mention that, west of the garden, the cave, and the spring was the old millrace tail from the now gone gristmill. The race tail is where the water runs after it has powered the mill. That old race was always filled with fresh spring water from springs that flowed into a small ravine and formed a run located behind the barn to the east of the main house. That ravine was an exciting place—one I will dedicate time to later.

The tenant house also had a chicken coop with a hog pen underneath. Besides the coop, there was a two-hole privy, known as "two-holer." I remember the lilac and mock orange bushes out in front of the house and a large elm tree that shaded the house as well as the coop; behind the house there were apple and pear trees.

It did, however, have one important drawback: it was in the flood-plain of Evitt's Creek, and on occasion, in the spring of the year, the creek would flood the bottom land, which included the tenant house. It was a problem, but not bad enough to get water into the house due to its position on a stone foundation at the higher end of the floodplain. If the water got too high, the tenant family would come up to the main house until the water receded. The tenants were always taken care of by Mom with whatever they needed until they could return home.

Besides having their house provided, our tenant farmers were paid forty dollars a month and provided with wood, coal, pigs, chickens, milk, butter, electricity, and one yearling cow a year. They were also allowed to hunt on the farm. Tenant farmers were an essential part of the farming that was done at Windale.

# Chapter 5

# A Working Farm

The type of farming Dad settled on was to raise white-faced Hereford cattle and the crops necessary to feed them. My father bought a purebred Hereford bull, which we called Curley, as well as some young heifers for breeding stock; he was now on his way. Now, you have to keep in mind that Dad was a grocery man not a farmer. To overcome this problem, he would read and study about what he wanted to do, what the best crops were for cattle, and how to plant, harvest, and store them, as well as how much to feed the livestock. Dad was a driven man, one who wanted to be successful and to do well at whatever he did. Dad used to read the magazine *Gentleman Farmer*, which was a good source of information for the type of farmer he was and the farming he wanted to do. My grandfather, his dad, labeled him "Gentleman Farmer," and it stuck. Even today, when I think of him, I remember him as the Gentleman Farmer; he never did any of the farm work, just gave the orders to get it done.

When Dad first started farming, I wasn't old enough to really help with much, but it was an exciting time. We started out with two work-horses—really big draft horses named King and Queen. King was bigger than Queen, but Queen was smarter than King, which when teamed up lead to King doing all the work. Queen would pace herself just far enough behind King to appear to be pulling, with her head down and breathing hard, but she was actually just walking along with him. It didn't take long for whoever was working with them to figure out what she was up to and tap her on the butt with the reins just enough to have her keep up the pace, but you had to stay alert or she would revert to her old habits quickly.

The first few years we farmed, everything was done with the horses: the plowing, planting, and harvesting. We used horses for cutting hay, raking it with dump rakes, and when necessary, tedding it and then moving it on wagons to the barns or places where it was to be staked. Without a tractor, there was no such thing as bailing hay.

The horses were also used to spread manure by pulling a manure spreader. I remember those heavy leather harnesses they wore and hooking them up to equipment with a single- or double-tree hookup. They were hardworking beasts of burden, but they were well taken care of. For three seasons of the year, they worked pretty regularly, but during the winter, there was very little for them to do with the type of farming we did, so it was their time to rest. They were mostly fed timothy hay and oats.

When not working, the horses were very passive animals but always had a mind of their own. I remember a number of times when I was feeding oats to King I had to walk into the stall beside him to dump the oats. King would lean over onto me when I got to about his belly, squeezing me against the stall boards between he and Queen's stall, just enough to trap me, but not enough to hurt me. His big eye was always looking at me when I got stuck; it was probably my imagination, but that eye kind of glistened. Another time, he waited until I got up to the manger, then gently stepped on my foot and held me there for a spell while he finished his oats. I guess he wanted to let me know he was a bigger man than me, or maybe he just wanted me to be there with him. I always trusted him even though he was so much bigger than me. He was so big I couldn't even see over his back, but then, I was probably only eight or ten years old. I remember I had to climb up on him to curry his back and butt; the rest I could do from the ground. King just loved to be brushed and curried.

Queenie was a different story. I didn't trust her, and she knew it. She would take every opportunity to scare me; maybe she didn't like the relationship I had with King. For example, she would always give me a hard time when I had to harness her up or brush or curry her. I guess I didn't like her and she didn't like me, but somehow we got through it all.

One day after I was old enough to work with the horses, I had Queen hooked up to the dump rake and was raking hay on Ruthella (Smouse) Faye's farm, just west of our farm on the other side of Evitt's Creek. I was raking to the east and west and dumping windrows to the north and south. Because of the shape of the field, it made for long windrows to pick up with the hay wagon. Things had been going quite well when all of a sudden Queen put her ears back and began running in a full-out gallop. Needless to say, I had no idea what was going on and tried to stop her; she would have none of it and kept running.

If you have never seen a dump hay rake, I need to explain. Hay rakes are made of solid steel and cast iron. They are very heavy, with a steel seat in the middle that is also very hard. When the rake took off on the rough ground, it was all I could do to stay on it. I couldn't get her to stop by pulling both reins, so I pulled on just one to turn her head to her neck, thinking that if she couldn't see where she was going, she would stop running. That didn't work, either. About that time, I noticed that there were bees around her; evidently, she had stepped in a yellow jacket's nest, and they were after her, stinging her   thus the running.

A dump rake could be set to dump manually or automatically. It would dump automatically by selecting a gear that is driven off the wheel, setting the dump according to how heavy the cut of hay is. In some fields, the windrows would be far apart, and in others, they would be close. I had it on automatic dumping. The windrows I had been making were quite close, and with the speed I was traveling, the rake was dumping in rapid succession, like a machine gun. The rake was dumping so hard that, when rising, the rakes were hitting the bottom of my seat, which made it even harder for me to stay on.

The situation was getting pretty grave. I looked up to see where we were going and saw a barbed wire fence coming up real fast. What to do? I decided right then that the only way to save the horse and myself was to let her go and to jump off the back of the rake. I knew I had to get off as soon as possible, so I let go of the reins and jumped. I had the presence of mind to remember what Coach Hawn, of Fort Hill High School, had taught me in gym class. When you hit the ground, tuck and roll, and boy, did I roll! Aside from some bruises, scratches, and a bump on the head, I was disoriented, but OK.

When I let go of the reins on Queenie, she saw the fence coming up very quickly, so she immediately turned to the right at high speed. The inertia generated by the rake caused it to flip over wheel to wheel, breaking the shaves and releasing Queenie so she wasn't pulled over, or worse, dragged through the fence. She ran for a while and finally stopped about a hundred yards from me, with shaves and harness in tow. I was so angry at what had happened I walked home and left the horse standing in the field. About an hour later, when it came time to eat, she showed up in the front yard in full harness, still dragging the shaves and the reins.

That evening when my father got home and heard about the incident with the rake, he was really upset with me. Upset with me! I couldn't understand why he wasn't upset with Queenie; she caused the problem, not me. He said I should have kept her under control. I thought to myself, *Queenie isn't a mule, she is a horse, and I'm only eleven years old. I would have loved to see you bouncing around on that seat trying to keep Queenie under control.* That's the first time of many that I realized my father wasn't perfect.

I must say this, though; it wasn't too long after that that my dad bought a tractor. It was an old used Oliver Row Crop, but it was a tractor and it wouldn't run off with me. Sadly, I wasn't home when the team was sold, so I never had a chance to say good-bye to King, and that really hurt me. I truly loved that old horse, and I really would have loved to look into one of those big eyes of his and tell him so.

# Chapter 6

# Feed Crops

In those days, the only way to make cattle farming work was to raise your own hay and feed. The tenant farmers whom my father hired did this. There were four fields dedicated to feed and hay only; the rest was used for pasture. Once in a while, if the growing season was really good, we would use some of the pastureland for hay, but mostly, we would rotate the four other fields between hay types and feed. The main feed we raised for the cattle was corn. The hay crops were timothy (because of the horses), orchard grass, mammoth clover, and sometimes a mixture of other grasses.

The corn crop was easy; we would fertilize it with manure before planting and cultivate it once or twice until it came time for the harvest. We never had a corn picker, so it was all done by hand. Once the shocks were brown and dry, we would take a wagon to the field and go down the rows and pick the ripe ears. It really wasn't a bad job; it just took a long time. You could pick a good-sized field in a day's time. The corn was then shoveled by hand into the corncrib for storage. Our crib was built up off the ground, with a wooden floor and wire-covered slats on the sides and back, and when it was empty, you could see through it, having a low-pitch roof on top. It was about ten feet wide and high, and about thirty feet long. Its design let plenty of air through the corn, yet kept it out of the weather.

Shortly after the first hard freeze, we would start feeding corn and hay to the cattle. In the beginning of winter before the snow arrived, the cattle would stay out in the pastures eating the last of the dried grasses. To feed them, I had to call them down to the barn or go get them. One of the tenant farmers taught me to call the herd so they would come every time. It was a strange call—it kind of sounded like *SICCC CAAFFF*—and you had to do it with a certain pitch and sound, repeating it over and over. The first part was called high and quick; the second part was called in a deep, throaty, long sound, with the *F* almost silent. It sounded like a mother cow would if calling a lost calf. It did work, and I was good at it. Even in the summer when we wanted to change pastures, I could call the herd, and they would come. Too bad it never worked that way with my kids!

The most rewarding time using the call was when the herd would get out and into someone else's pasture—or worse, in his or her yard—and I was able to call them in. Remember, I said "the herd." If one or two or even a few cattle got out, however, there was no calling them; it was as if, once through the fence, they became brain-dead and lost all sense of hearing. They had no sense of direction, they had no idea where they got out, and they had no intention of doing what I wanted them to do. Many times, I thought it would be a lot easier just to shoot them and drag them home with the tractor. Boy, I wonder what my father would have said about that! I have to say this, though; in later years, he seemed to be a little more understanding.

Speaking of cows getting out, it was a constant chore to keep the fences in working order. One of the first things I learned living on a cattle farm is how to build and fix a fence. We had miles of fence all over the farm, and when things were slow; I would hook up the small wagon to the horses—or later, the tractor—and start walking and inspecting the fence line. I had to have everything I needed in the wagon: a keg of staples, a roll of barbed wire, wire stretchers, an ax, a regular hand hammer, a sledgehammer, and a crosscut saw. The work mainly consisted of replacing staples or repairing a stretch that had gotten broken, but once in a while, a tree would fall and take the whole fence down. I then had to find posts in the woods—locust trees about four to five inches thick were best. Locust wood made great fence posts; it was very hard wood and took a long time to rot away. You could pound on it to drive it into the ground without it splitting, but it was very difficult to hammer staples into if it had cured; if it was green there was no problem. Before replacing the post, I would have to chop up the tree with the ax or cut the trunk with the crosscut saw, and then sharpen one end with the ax so it could be driven into the ground.

It was always best to have hired help when doing fence work, especially when using the crosscut saw or stretching a long strand of wire. I usually had my friend Novell "Norney" Gillum working with me. Norney was a good fence builder. We worked well together and always had a lot to talk about. If you built fences, you had to know how to build gates. We built our gates out of barbed wire by extending the three- or four-strand fence across an opening, then wrapping and stapling each strand to a post that was not driven into the ground. Next, a wire loop was stapled near the top of the post, and then slipped over the subsequent post, which had a wire loop at the bottom to secure the gate. The gate could then be opened if needed without any trouble. We built these easy-open-type gates all over the farm, so if the cattle got out, we had a place to run them back in until we found the breakout place. Most of the fence work took place in the winter or early spring, before the cattle were put back out to pasture.

Dad must have been reading about Angus cattle in that *Gentleman Farmer* magazine, because he decided to get some Black Angus cattle. It was when they were just becoming popular in the United States. Well, these cattle were like deer; I couldn't keep them in a pasture, because they always found their way out or simply jumped the fence. I spent many hours getting them back in and adding an extra wire to the top of the fence or building gates to try to contain them. For the most part, we eventually kept them where we wanted, but there were three that we could never get to stay fenced. One year, they even spent the winter in the woods. They became quite feral, so Dad decided to have them shot and sold to a butcher in Cumberland. I bet their meat was tough as shoe leather!

Getting back to the corn, it's best to grind up the corn when you feed it to cattle, so Dad bought what was called a hammer mill. Driven by a large, long belt, it was attached to the Oliver Row Crop 70 tractor that Dad purchased when the horses were sold. The belt was about twelve feet long, and when hooked to the tractor and hammer mill, it was twisted in the middle, which kept it from flying off the pulleys. I tell you, when in operation; this machine was the loudest thing I've ever heard. It's a wonder I can hear anything today; remember, it was called a hammer mill. Another thing, I didn't want to get anywhere near that belt when the tractor was running; if that belt ever got off and hit you, there wouldn't be too much left to pick up. To grind the corn, I would dump a bushel of corn—husk, cob, and all—into the throat, and wham, just like that it was ground corn. The ground corn was kept in burlap sacks tied with bailing twine and stored in the granary to be fed later to the cattle.

That's not the end of the corn story. Once a day in the winter months, we fed the cattle the ground corn in troughs at the feed barn, located behind the main barn. To make the feed more nutritional, we poured black molasses over it, which we stored in a large tank. It had a large spigot on it, and I would put a large handle bucket under it and fill it up. It worked great until it got really cold. Have you ever heard the phrase "As slow as cold molasses"? Well, I truly know what that means! Many a night at feeding time, I had to wait in the cold until that bucket was full, but sometimes, not too often, it would get so cold the molasses would not pour out of the tank, so we could not feed it. It was very dark molasses, bottom-of-the-barrel type, with a pungent odor—really nasty stuff, but sweet. The cattle loved it, and once we started feeding it in early winter, they couldn't wait to get into the barn. Sometimes it was pure chaos. They had plenty of hay to feed on, which they got twice a day, but there was no interest in that until the ground corn and molasses was devoured. As I said, some nights it wouldn't pour because of the cold, and when that happened, it was kind of risky going into the feed shed, as they expected it every night.

There are two things in particular I remember about feeding molasses. One is that, after the cattle had eaten the corn and molasses, their breath was so pungent it was enough to knock me over; the feed shed just reeked. The odor of that strong molasses was awful and permeated the whole barn. Of course, that odor mixed with that of the wet cow manure sure did clear out my sinuses. The other is a time I had just dumped the last bucket of molasses over the corn when one of the cows decided she was not going to let me out of the feeding shed. She lowered her head and shook two big horns at me; she meant business, and she was really big. Again, what to do? There wasn't much to consider, so I swung the bucket around my back, up over my head, and down onto those two large horns, where it stuck—well. With the bucket stuck on her horns, she forgot all about me, and I escaped to the main barn. All my dad had to say was, "You know those buckets cost money." Remember, I told you he wasn't much of a farmer.

# Chapter 7

# Making Hay

After the Oliver Row Crop came on the scene, making hay was still difficult work, but it took less time. It was not the toilsome job when done with the horses. All of the hay-making equipment had to be modified so the tractor could pull it; however, the job of making hay was done basically the same way. The equipment we used to cut hay was attached to the tractor by a three-point hitch and rode on two wheels. The power takeoff of the tractor was geared to a pitman rod that was mounted on a cam. The cam caused the rod to cycle back and forth. The pitman rod was hooked to a saw tooth-blade cutter bar via a ball-and-joint arrangement that cycled back and forth with the pitman rod. It in turn was slotted into a cutter bar carriage with guards to protect the blades. The cutter bar carriage had an arm on its end to fold the cut hay away from the next cut.

The machine worked pretty well except for a few things. The blades would get dull quickly, and the rivets holding them on would break or come loose often. The biggest problem was the blades sometimes jammed, causing the pitman rod to break. Pitman rods were made of seasoned oak or hickory wood and were not changed easily. Many times, I went up to the sawmill located on Bedford Road behind the volunteer fire company to have new ones made; if my memory serves me right, the sawmill was called Valley Lumber. I remember usually getting two made at a time because they broke often. It was a complicated machine for its time but was much better than using a handheld mowing scythe to do the job.

As I said earlier, all of our hay was taken up by hand using three-pronged pitchforks, then loaded onto wagons in the field. If I was on the wagon, it was my responsibility to stack it properly by laying it out correctly and tramping it down, so when it came time to unload it, it came off in layers. The wagon was pulled down the middle of two windrows; if they were close, there would be two people throwing it up on the wagon and two people placing it and tramping it down. The best job was driving the tractor, which was usually done by my sister Christina. We had to have extra help during hay time, and usually, it came from locals of the surrounding area. Besides the tenant farmer who worked the farm, some of the extra help may have been his children, my sister Christina, and kids from around the neighborhood—I guess anyplace we could find it. All those we hired got paid ten cents an hour. Everyone got paid but Chris and me—imagine that!

Once the hay was stacked on the wagon, it was moved to one of two places down by the lower barn near the tenant house to be built into stacks or tossed into the haymow of the barn east of the main house. The process of building haystacks required four people—two to toss the hay on the stack and two to place it and tramp it down. Placing the hay after it was thrown onto the stack was the best job; we didn't have all that hay chaff falling back on us after the toss. After the wagon was empty, we would comb down the sides of the stack with our pitchforks to make it smooth so rainwater would run off and not damage the hay later. Sometimes there were two hay wagons working, so building stacks was an ongoing project.

I loved building those stacks. When finished, the perfect mounds of hay stood as a tribute to our efforts. We usually built three at that site, and in the winter, if we looked down there on a cold, cold morning, we would see steam rising out of the top of the stacks. They kind of looked like big round chimneys. What a beautiful sight—one I will never forget and will always be in my mind's eye.

Making haystacks and haying in general may seem a simple task to most, but it really wasn't; there is a system to doing it correctly and a skill needed to do it right, especially when building stacks. If the stacks were built wrong, the entire hay crop could be lost, and without the hay, the animals would starve or suffer needlessly.

Most of us didn't wear shirts when working in the hay fields because of the heat, so we were covered with chaff, which really made you itch. It was a dry job too. I remember one year when a few of us decided to try chewing tobacco to keep our mouths moist, at the urging of the tenant farmer who chewed all the time. I believe the tobacco was Red Man Chewing Tobacco. What a mistake! Most of us got sick. I'm sure he got a chuckle out of it, though. That was the last time I ever had a chew.

Making hay was a long day, lasting from early morning, as soon as the hay was dry, until late in the evening when the dew started to set in. When we were done, we would all go to one of three swimming holes on Evitt's Creek. The cool, clear water would wash all that dirt and chaff off us and sooth the itching. One hole was just below the house; it was small but the closest one if the day was late. The second was also on my dad's property, located about a mile from the house at the big wooden bridge over Evitt's Creek on Mason Road, just below the old one-room schoolhouse.

Much bigger and deeper, this hole was used by a lot of people, especially on weekends. Folks would come from all over to spend Saturday or Sunday at the creek. They would bring picnic lunches, go swimming, and wash their cars—just make a day of it. Another great thing used to happen at this swimming hole. Every once in a while, one of the churches in the area would have services at the creek and baptize people right there in the water. We kids used to sit up on the railing of the big bridge and watch it all happen. Some of those folks were fully dressed and would walk down into the creek with the preacher, who was also fully dressed. He would hold them, bend them back until they were fully submerged, then raise them up and bless them. Some of the people cried, and some hugged others on the bank; it was really a sight to see. I didn't think of it too much then, but that was really a wonderful thing that happened there. Sometimes I wish it had happened to me.

The third swimming hole was the Fagan's' swimming hole. To get there, we had to travel by bike a couple of miles from the house, past the wooden bridge, and across one of the fields below the Fagan's' home. It was the greatest. There was deep water and lots of it as well as a tree with three places to jump off—a low, medium, and high branch. There was a gradually sloping bank to get into the water that had been fixed up by people who swam there, plenty of room to park our bicycles, and even a place where the girls could spread a blanket or towel if they desired.

I can remember the first day I got up enough courage to jump from the high branch of the tree. I had climbed up there other times but could not muster the courage to jump and dejectedly had to climb back down. It was about a twenty-foot drop, but that day it looked like a hundred. Well, when I finally jumped, I didn't hit the water too well and smacked my left leg a little bit, but that didn't matter. I had done it, and when I came up out of the water, people actually cheered. Wow, we all knew that it was a big deal and a rite of passage of some sort. What great times they were, with such feelings of friendship, freedom, acceptance, satisfaction, and the pride of a job well done. The lessons I learned those summers are still with me; they became part of my character, my person, my life spirit. Doing that work taught me many of life's lessons: do it right the first time, take care of those things that need taken care of, respect the animals that work for you, learn to share the job burden with others, work in harmony with others, and most of all, understand that nature is our provider and should be treated with respect.

# Chapter 8

# Tenant Farmers

For reasons I didn't understand at the time, the tenant farmers didn't usually stay too long. We had them on the farm for about ten or so years, and during that time, there were four families that I can remember and one single older man, who was the last one we hired. For the most part, they were simple people who lived close to the land. I spent a lot of time with them, either working with the man of the house or playing with their children.

I remember one family that I got to know quite well when I was younger. Frank was the name of the man who worked the farm, and his wife's name was Lizzie, probably Elizabeth; I don't remember their last name. Frank was a middle-aged man who had had a great deal of experience farming. Frank came along after we switched over from the horses to the tractor; actually, he may have been there when that happened, but I'm not sure.

Frank was easy to talk to about anything. He didn't mind answering my questions and listening to my chatter about things that young boys talk about, as I'm sure he was used to it at home. Frank took the time to show me how to do whatever he was doing, and I was eager to learn. I remember one time when he showed me how to use a mowing scythe; it was almost bigger than I, but I wanted to learn. We were cleaning the grass away from around the springhouse. It was a small job, and I guess he thought it would be a good place for me to learn. I got a few swipes in, and he said, "Now I'm going to show you how to sharpen it; then you'll be able to use it yourself when you want." A dull blade just didn't work and generated a lot of extra work.

To sharpen the scythe, he stood it up on the end of the handle and held the blade in one hand at the top. Then with a rounded whetstone in the other hand, he ran it down one side of the blade and up the other in a rhythmic motion. Well, it looked simple enough to me. With the rhythm, it only took a few swipes to sharpen it up. Frank then asked me if I would be OK to finish the job, and of course, I told him I would be fine. You never want to let your teacher know that you didn't quite understand everything that was said.

I guess I was about halfway through when the blade started to hang up, so I stopped, got the whetstone out of my pocket, and began to sharpen the blade. Things were going fine until I got a little too confident or maybe got out of rhythm, and in the process of making the downward stroke with the whetstone, I slid my left thumb along the cutting edge of the blade. It sliced the inside of my thumb about a quarter of an inch deep as well as my thumbnail. It really didn't hurt, but blood was everywhere. I wasn't too far from the house, so I ran down there. Mom fixed me up with some BFI powder and bandaged me up so I could finish the job.

I never told Frank what happened, but I'm sure he figured it out when he saw my thumb. He never said anything about it to me; he probably didn't want to embarrass me or hurt my pride, as that's the kind of person he was. He taught me most everything I know about farming. He made sure I understood how to maintain all the equipment and how to use it properly. He taught me how to milk and feed all the animals, when crops were ready for harvest, when was the best time to cut the hay, and how to build and repair fences. Frank was also the guy who taught me how to call cattle. I really admired him and followed him everywhere.

I was always welcome in Frank's home, especially in their kitchen, where Lizzie was always cooking something on the stove. Most times, there was a pot of beans on the stove with some type of varmint meat in it, and it smelled so good. My pallet was introduced to many different types of wild game at Frank's table—deer, coon, possum, muskrat, rabbit, and squirrel—and I ate it all, mainly in stew. We surely didn't eat that type of food at Windale, although we did have squirrel potpie once in a while when my grandmother Windish would make it.

I had many lunches there and quite a few dinners. I also got to use their privy, which I thought was neat; it was different sitting there on that wooden seat and using the Sears catalog. My mother never objected to me eating there—I had a free reign when it came to that. I did mess up one time, though, when I went to eat dinner at the tenant house and forgot it was Mom's birthday. I caught it about that and heard about it for many years to come; it kind of became family folklore.

We didn't have a garden at home because Dad brought home all the fresh vegetables we needed from the store, so Frank let me help with theirs. I developed an interest and desire to do gardening as a result of that opportunity, which served me well when I had a family of my own. The tenant farmers knew how to provide for themselves, and that always intrigued me.

There was a tradition in Western Maryland of butchering a hog on New Year's Day that Frank and his family followed. He and some of his relatives would start the day by killing the hog and then spent the rest of the day processing it. Most of the hog was made into hams or bacon; all the fat was rendered down into lard, with what was left becoming crackling. Nothing was wasted. Some of the pig was pickled, some made into scrapple, and the tenderloin was generally roasted over an open flame and eaten that day or shared with others to take home. It was an experience that I have never had since.

Frank was a teacher—a patient man and a humble man. His family always came first, and he treated me as such. Being with him and his family gave me the ability and confidence to talk to and respect others, regardless of their station in life. I learned how to accept the simple gifts that life provides and how to enjoy them. I wish I could thank him for all he taught me and for welcoming me into his home. So many times in our life, we don't realize how much some people have done for us until it's too late. When they decided to leave the farm, I missed him for a long time; I guess I loved him and grieved about his leaving, and as I'm writing this, I still feel that grief in my heart.

Then there was Russ. Russ was a much younger man than Frank who came to Windale after Frank left but didn't work for us too long. He was unlike anyone I had never encountered before. He had a young wife and a new baby. Russ had a lot of crazy ideas, which sometimes worked and sometimes didn't. He was a storyteller, mainly about himself. I'm sure many of the stories were somewhat true, but most were fantasies that he envisioned for himself. A lot of the stories were about his escapades with women. I was, at that time and age, just beginning to understand what all that meant, so I took it all in as the gospel truth. When he got into one of his stories, his eyes would light up, and he would go into great detail about the event.

For his age, he seemed to know what he was doing as far as the farm was concerned, but sometimes I suspected that he believed in some of the fantasies he talked about. Once, he told me he knew how to lead two hogs like a team of horses. Dad had told him to move two of our hogs from behind the upper barn down to the lower barn. These two hogs weighed about one hundred and fifty pounds apiece, but they were used to people and not wild. Normally, we would run them up a shoot onto a wagon with high sides and move them wherever they were needed—not a difficult task. Russ, however, told me he could rope up these hogs in such a way as to lead them as a team down to the other barn, so he proceeded to put a rope on the left front leg of one hog and the right front leg of the second hog. The rope was then placed under them and up by the opposite side. The two hogs now being side by side and with Russ holding the two ropes, he said all he had to do was pull the rope if one got out of line and the leg would collapse. That way the hogs could be controlled and lead anywhere.

So Russ told me to open the gate to the hog pen, and out came Russ holding the two ropes with the hogs walking side by side. Down the lane he went, walking the two pigs. All went well for a while, until one of the hogs decided it didn't want to go along with the arrangement anymore. Russ pulled on the rope, but nothing happened, and I guess the rest of the story is clear—the hogs took off, with him running after them. Russ spent a great deal of time over the remainder of the day catching the hogs and getting them down to the other barn.

Russ did another crazy thing one time—and I stress *one* time—when he needed to move a young calf from the upper barn to the lower barn. We were inside the barn, with the big front door closed. Russ tied a rope around the calf's neck and the other end of it around his waist, then told me to open the door, which moved by rollers on a steel track. When I opened the door, the calf took off at a fast run. There was just enough slack in the rope to let him get up to speed, and when he hit the end of the rope, Russ became airborne. Russ ran for a while but was quickly overtaken by the speed of the calf, which dragged him down the driveway before giving up. I ran after both of them, but there wasn't anything I could do. Needless to say, besides hurting his pride, Russ had some pretty bad brush burns and scratches from the cinder driveway.

I never forgot that guy, with his crazy antics and unusual approach to life. Russ was so different from Frank. He wasn't what I would call a teacher, surely not a mentor; he just provided a different perspective on how to live life. My focus, however, was in a different direction, but it is always good to know what kind of people you're going to bump into out there and know how to relate to them.

# Chapter 9

# Rats!

My Father read an article in one of his *Gentleman Farmer* magazines claiming that when it came to feeding cattle in the wintertime, you could kill two birds with one stone, so to speak, with a labor-saving process that provided improved nourishment. The article stated that if you planted oats and let them grow just to the brink of maturity and harvested the entire plant with the oats still attached, they could then be fed to the livestock, which would benefit from the combination of hay and grain.

It all sounded good to Dad, so the following spring, we plowed the upper field, about fifteen or so acres, and planted oats. It was an uneventful crop; we just had to watch to make sure we harvested it at the brink of maturity, as the article said. The harvest came off without a hitch, and the loose, not baled, oat hay was stored in the haymow over the upper barn for the winter feeding. By fall, however, a small problem began to emerge—hints of things to come. We often had barn owls in the mow from time to time, but that had changed—now we had them all the time. I also noticed a lot of chaff falling through the cracks in the mow floor, which doesn't happen with just hay. The real telltale sign was the rustling that took place in the mow.

Rats had been around the barn before, but in limited numbers. Rats are smart creatures; they only produce enough young that their food resources are able to provide for. Well, guess what? We had provided a lot more food resources for them, and they were in a hurry to produce as many young as they could to try to eat all those oats that were in the mow. It was unbelievable. No matter where you went in the barn, you would see a rat scurry away. Rats are great diggers; they started to undermine everything they could find that was undermineable. They didn't just live in the mow; they were under the granary, the cabinetry, the box stables where the horses were housed, in the tractor shed—just everywhere. The setup was just great for them. They had plenty of food and room, and there was a small run just outside the barn, so they had plenty of water. Dad recognized we had a real problem, but nothing could be done until the hay was fed to the cattle the next winter, which was still a couple of months off. So while we waited, the rat population just got bigger.

Finally, we started to feed the oat hay, which by that time was more hay than oats. Well, once the oats were gone, we had all these rats with no food to eat, so they started to migrate to other sources, like the corncrib and the chicken house, down the run to our house, farther down the run to the tenant house and their chicken coop, and even farther down to the lower barn. Only God knows where the rest of them went. Rats just don't leave; there isn't any pied piper to get rid of them, so we had to figure a way to dispose of them ourselves.

You may recall that I mentioned my friend Norney, who lived up on Bedford Road. I guess I was about thirteen, and Norney was a year or so older than I. Anyway, one day, Norney and I were talking about the rat problem. We had been shooting some rats with our .22 rifles when we could, but weren't beginning to put a dent in their population, and besides, it was dangerous to be shooting around the barn with all the livestock in the vicinity. Dad would have had my hide if I shot a cow or, heaven forbid, a horse.

We recognized that the chicken coop was now the biggest problem. The rats were eating all the scratch feed and laying mash they could every day, and things were looking bleak for the chickens. The rats were living under the coop, and despite the fact that the coop was made of solid oak, they had gnawed holes into it wherever they could to get in at night when the door was closed. During the day, the coop was always open so the chickens could free range. In the winter, if the weather was really bad, we wouldn't let them out, but most of the time, they were free to come and go as they pleased.

What a mess! What to do? Well, Norney and I hit on this plan to solve the chicken coop rat problem. First, we sealed up all the gnawed holes with tin can lids, which left only one large hole that we couldn't close up, and that was the corner of the door to the coop. Having completed covering the holes, we placed our .22 rifles in the coop with an ample supply of .22 shorts and then waited for dark. Our chickens were well trained, and by dark, they were all in the coop and at rest on their roosts. I guess I should mention that I had not cleared this activity with Dad, but I figured that if we got rid of the rat problem, only praise would follow.

Well, as we suspected upon approaching the coop and after giving the rats ample time to get in the coop, it sounded like a banquet was going on in there. The rest of the plan was to work as follows: We would charge the coop as fast as we could—remember, it was dark.

Norney would go in first and switch on the lights, and I would follow, closing the door and quickly jamming a rag into the hole we were unable to close up earlier. Once this was done, we would be in the coop with all the rats, and it would be only a matter of time until we could shoot them all and be rid of the problem.

We both charged the coop, Norney leading the way up the steps. He hit the light switch, and the first thing we hadn't expected happened. There were two switches on the wall, the switch box type—one was for the lights, and the other was to shut off all the power to the coop. I said, "Norney, turn on the lights," and he replied, "The switch doesn't work." You guessed it; Norney had hit the wrong switch, so there was no light. I then said, "Turn them both on." Remember, my job was to close the door and stuff a rag into the hole at the bottom of the door, but it was very dark, and with all the confusion, I couldn't find the hole right away.

By that time, the rats had figured out what was going on and were all headed for the door. There I was on my knees in the chicken manure trying to stuff the darn rag into the hole, and the rats were all trying to get out through that same hole. I had rats running all over me—up and over my back, between my legs, and over my hands. I hollered at Norney, "Get the lights on!" But still, no lights. Finally, I got up after closing off the hole with the rag and got the lights on. Man, there were rats running everywhere, so Norney and I ran to our rifles, loaded up, and began the big kill.

Having a well-built coop made of solid oak presented another problem. When we fired our rifles, most of the bullets would ricochet and fly around the coop, which made both Norney and me very apprehensive. The chickens were becoming very nervous as well. I don't know if you have ever seen roosting chickens when they are suddenly exposed to a lot of light and noise, but they become very confused and kind of stretch out their necks and blink a lot. I'm sure they had expected to spend a restful night on the roost, but instead, they were exposed to rifle shots and full daylight. Anyway, Norney and I decided that, in order to avoid the ricochets, we would stand behind the two steel feed barrels in the corner and shoot the rats from there. Now that I think about it, even behind the barrels was still a stupid idea, and of course, it didn't help the chickens much. Well, when all was said and done, we had a bushel of dead rats, Norney and I were unscathed by the ricochets, and there were no dead chickens.

The next morning, I took the bushel of dead rats up the hill to the upper forty and dumped them in the field for the buzzards, which, by the way, devoured them all by the following day. With the exception of a few bones, the rats were completely turned into buzzards, or maybe coons, or foxes, or whatever. When Dad came home from work that evening, I explained that Norney and I had gotten rid of all the rats in the chicken coop and that there shouldn't be a problem anymore. He didn't say much, but my grandfather got a real kick out of the story. I figured we had done well.

Then another problem started to rear its ugly head. In the ensuing weeks, egg production began to drop off sharply; actually, it stopped all together. That's when, I guess you could say, the ship hit the sand with Dad. By the sound of things, Dad would have rather had the rats than no eggs. I'm sure that was not the case; he was just concerned about a lot of customers at the store who had to find another source for their eggs for a while. But all's well that ends well. In a few more weeks, the egg production was back to normal. I learned a valuable lesson with that rat project: chickens don't like rifle shots disturbing their rest.

# Chapter 10

# Chickens

That chicken coop was the center of a number of good family stories. In the summertime when it was light well into the evening, my family used to sit outside on the front porch after dinner to talk about the day. It was a great way for the whole family to be together, and it was always comfortable in the evening. The porch had an old trumpet vine that grew up the west side of it, all the way up to the portico, which completely blocked the late-day sun. By the way, that vine is still there all these years later. Because of the flowers, the vine always had ruby-throated humming birds buzzing around it constantly. One evening, my grandfather Windish was sitting next to the vine when a humming bird flew by and went into a flower right next to him. He calmly reached over and plucked it out of the flower. I was amazed and got my first close-up look at one of those fast flyers. After a few minutes, he just opened his hand and let it fly away.

We kids used to run around outside as children do—catching lightning bugs, lying in the grass, watching the stars come out, listening to what the old folks had to say, and just waiting for the end of the day. It was just a great time that I have many fond memories of. You know those memories that are tucked away in the corner of your heart that will always come back to you on warm summer nights years later? I remember my kids doing the same thing, and I was right out there with them in my heart.

Anyway, every evening, just about dark, it was time to go up to the chicken coop and close the door to keep out the night prowlers. There were many critters that would go into the coop during the night if you didn't close it up—weasels, foxes, coons, skunks, mink, or whatever could do harm in there. There was always a discussion among us kids as to whose turn it was to walk the fifty yards up to the coop to close the door. I'm sure it wasn't the distance as much as the darkness.

One night, I believe it was my sister Chris who had the honor of closing the door; however, it had gotten late, and she took the flashlight with her to assist her on her way. She hadn't gotten too far before she came running back, screaming something about red eyes. She had evidently shown the light into the eyes of some critter coming out of the coop, and they had shown red. As I remember, I was then assigned to go up and close the door. Light in hand, somewhat apprehensive, I went up, but I didn't see any eyes and closed the door. From then on, there was seldom a night when one of us was instructed to close up to the coop that my grandfather Windish wouldn't say, "Watch out for old red eye." It was just enough to put that little bit of fear into us when we walked up that dark barn road to the coop.

Another night, I was going up to close the coop when I saw an animal run out of the coop and under it into a pile of old wood. Being the smart guy I was, I went back to the house to get my shotgun—

a twenty-gauge Remington pump loaded with number six shot—and then went up to the coop to get rid of whatever critter was in there and no doubt up to no good. It was almost dark when I got back to the coop with my weapon. Shining my flashlight, I could see the eyes of a critter hiding in the pile of wood under the coop, so I drew up and fired. I'm sure the folks on the porch were quite startled when they heard that blast; I hadn't told anyone what I was doing, which usually got me into trouble. I can hear my father now saying, "What the hell was that?" and my grandfather, his dad, saying, "Oh, that was only George up at the coop."

Well, I got the critter, and you guessed it, it was a skunk. As soon as the odor hit me, I knew I was in deep trouble. The barn and the coop sat in a natural hollow east of the house, about fifty yards away. In the summertime, that hollow, which ran a good mile or so up behind the barn, would cool off real quick, and that nice cool air would flow down to the house and cool things down just great. This particular evening, however, and for a few more to come, that nice cool air flowing down from the barn hollow brought the pungent order of skunk. After realizing what I had done, I hollered to everyone to get in the house and close the windows, as the smell was getting really bad. Again, my dad wasn't too happy with me; there were threats of taking my gun away. The next day, I got rid of the dead skunk and had it turned into buzzard, as with the rats, but we had to deal with the smell for while, and there wasn't any porch sitting for the rest of the week. Weeks later, we would still occasionally get a whiff of "Evening in Paris" skunk aroma. This time my shotgun blast didn't stop the chickens from laying their eggs every day, though, for which I was thankful.

Chickens were always a part of our farm plan. We would gather dozens of eggs every day to be sold later at Dad's store in downtown

Cumberland. We tried to gather the eggs twice a day, once about ten in the morning and then again in the late afternoon. Except for weekends or summertime, Mom got the eggs in the morning, and I or my sister Chris got them after school. Our chickens, Rhode Island Reds, laid brown eggs. Besides selling them at the store, we all had them for breakfast nearly every morning, and being a large family, it took a lot of eggs.

Gathering eggs wasn't a big deal, but some of the old hens didn't want to be disturbed while they were on the nest. If we weren't careful, they would give us a good peck on the hand, sometimes drawing blood. I got wise to these old birds quickly and figured out how to avoid the peck. If I distracted them with one hand, I could grab them by the neck with my free hand, then gather the eggs from under them. One really neat thing I used to do was to wait until a hen was just about ready to drop her egg, and then I would reach into the nest, hold my hand under her rear end, and catch the warm egg as it dropped. When an egg is first laid, it is not hard like the ones bought in a store; it is soft and somewhat pliable. In a short time, after being exposed to the air, it becomes hard.

Every so often, I would have the dubious duty of being told to catch a chicken and prepare it for Mom so she could cook it for dinner. It sounds like a nasty job, but that's how it was done then, and we didn't think of it in the way people think of it today. After chopping off its head, I would let it run or flip around until it died. Then came the part I disliked most—dunking it into a bucket of boiling water and then pulling off the hot feathers. Boy, did they smell bad! I then had to pick the pin feathers off the skin, and after that, I would dress the bird out just like with any other animal I butchered. It was always worth it, though, when the bird was served at dinner.

Dad had a friend that ran Clopper Oil Company in LaVale, Maryland, and somehow they got together on a deal to raise a new breed of chicken called Corocks—probably something that Dad read in a *Gentleman Farmer* magazine article. Supposedly, when they were mature fryers, they would be all white meat. Dad and his friend were the planners, and I worked the plan. The chicks arrived in late winter in five large cardboard boxes with about one hundred in each box. It was still cold, so we had set up a large brooder at the south end of the chicken coop. It looked rather like a large roof with a low pitch that stood very close to the floor. From the edge hung canvas curtains, and inside were numerous light bulbs for heat, small feeders, and Mason jar water dispensers. The chicks were only a few days old when they arrived, so I had to watch them closely. When not in school, I spent most of my time in the coop watching over them. I did my homework there many nights. I really loved to watch them dart in and out of the brooder. With baby chicks, a few always die, but as I remember, we didn't lose too many.

In about twelve or fourteen weeks, they were ready to be moved outside to free range. Dad had five portable coops built that moved on skids. Each coop had a feeder inside and a water supply on the side. They could be moved with the tractor via a hook and eye on the front. They had tin roofs with wire around the sides. Each had a door in the front that could be closed at night. My job was to provide food and water and move the coops around when needed; oh, and I had to close the coops up at night and open them in the morning. Once I got the routine down, it didn't take much of my time. Things went well, and they weren't much care.

One day, Dad arrived with a new feed for me to give them. It came in cardboard boxes and was a solid block of something the consistency of corn meal mush. It was a gray-yellow color and very heavy. I was told it was some new high-powered feed that had hormones, vitamins, and minerals in it—everything the chickens would need. After a few weeks, some strange things started to happen. For example, some of the birds would grow one leg longer than the other; some got full feathers, while others didn't; some couldn't get up, and others just died. I lost a lot of birds before it was over at the end of the summer, and they were sent to the butcher to be processed.

Today, when I think about that incident, I have mixed emotions. It was a great learning experience for me. I ran the whole project, and I was in charge of making it a success, which forced me to be responsible at a young age. I also learned that you are not always in control of what is happening around you. Others can affect your successes, and there isn't anything you can do about it, except learning from it and trying to avoid those situations in the future. Another important lesson I learned from the project and from also dealing with farm animals is to be compassionate to those animals that are under your control and to care for them as God would have you care for them. I will never forget that we are the stewards of all living things and that they should be cared for and used as they were intended, not exploited for personal gain or greed.

I also learned that there can be unseen rewards in life, things you don't expect for things you have done, and that sometimes others recognize your accomplishments without you ever telling them about it. I was a member of 4-H for many years while growing up. We had a meeting every month in the old schoolhouse down Union Grove Road just past the Union Grove Campground on the other side of the road. Attending 4-H was a good experience. We learned many things from the county agent, who always gave us a talk and showed us a film.

That old schoolhouse was kind of neat too; it had an old potbelly stove that kept us warm in the winter and was basically still the same old schoolhouse that had been used to educate many of the local kids over the years. It can still be visited today, as it has been restored and is open to the public on occasion.

Well, to continue with the reward story, evidently my 4-H leader, who was the county agent for our area, was aware of my project and entered it at the fair without my knowledge. The project won first place, and I received a gold chicken pin for my effort. Now, before you laugh at the "chicken pin," please remember I was just a farm boy who hadn't seen too much reward in his life, and that pin was a big deal to me. I kept that pin for a lot of years, but when Mom sold the house after Dad died in 1963, it disappeared. If I had it today, I just might wear it once in a while, just so someone would ask me about it. You have to be proud of all you do in this life, whether it be large or small, and don't let others take away the pleasures those accomplishments provide. That project gave me confidence that I could do what I needed to do and be able to do it well.

As I have mentioned before, my dad never told me that I had done a good job, but over time, he did give me more and more responsibility, on the farm and at the store, as I grew in knowledge and ability. I understand it now, yet it was difficult not understanding and not having him tell me at the time. I also realize now that, in his mind, he had a plan for my development and my education that was more than I could have imagined then.

# Chapter 11

# Best Friends

Besides the chickens and cattle on the farm, we had ducks, geese, pigs, cats, and dogs. Dogs would come and go, but I remember one in particular named Donny. He was a cross between a bulldog and a cocker spaniel. His body was really mixed up. He had bowlegs in the front and a big chest like a bulldog, but the rest of his body was built like a spaniel. He was a great pet and was always with me. The only time I made him stay at home was when I was working on the farm using mowing equipment; I surely didn't want to cut him up. Like most good dogs, though, he didn't understand; he wanted to be with me.

He lived a long time, about fourteen years. I was in college and had come home for the summer to work in the store, and one day, I couldn't find him anywhere, so I went looking for him, calling his name, but got no response. I finally found him in the run, lying in the cool spring water, and I knew something was wrong. As it turned out, he had contracted distemper and died the next day. My heart was broken; I had lost my best friend. I used to talk to him as we would travel around the farm or up to the barn; he was my buddy when I was alone. There was a hill east of the house where I buried him, good and deep so nothing would dig him up. I then went down to the creek and dug up a young sycamore sapling and planted it on his grave. Today that sycamore is huge (about fifty or sixty feet tall), healthy, and still growing—it's just beautiful. Mary Miltenberger, who now owns the farm, dubbed it the "Donny Tree." It is great knowing that Donny is now part of the magnificent tree. Whenever I return to the house, I go up to his grave and that great tree to see him and say hi.

We had another dog, Timmy, a full-blooded cocker. We got Timmy from George Rule, who owned the photography studio on Center Street in Cumberland, not far from Stacey's Market. Timmy was a duck killer and didn't last too long. Mom gave him away to a guy that came to the farm to buy hay.

I had another dog, Independence, or Indy for short; his birthday was on the Fourth of July. He was a collie and good dog, but he was no Lassie. Indy had a real problem with ticks, and he got Rocky Mountain Tick fever, which caused him to lose control of the left side of his face. He looked absolutely pitiful with his cheek, lip, and eye drooping down. My grandfather used to sit on the porch in the evening and pick ticks off Indy, and Indy would just sit there and not move, as if he knew that Pop was trying to help him. One time, Pop was tugging at what he thought was a tick, and Indy was struggling to stay put and endure the pain. Well, it turned out that Pop was trying to pull off one of his tits. After that incident, Dad decided that Indy should be trimmed each summer to help keep the ticks off. So each year after that, Indy would have all his fur sheared off, with the exception of the end of his tail. He looked funny, like a short-haired lion; just imagine a collie with no hair. Every spring when he got his buzz cut, he would hide in the barn for a few days without coming down to the house. I guess he was embarrassed, but eventually, he would show up at the house with his head down, mope around a few more days, and then was back to his old self.

Indy loved to chase cars. We would be sitting on the porch when a car would come up the road, and he would take off like a shot, dash across the yard, and chase the car as it went around the curve. He was a real nuisance! The problem was he was fast enough to catch up with the cars, making people very nervous. My dad said it had to stop, so we came up with the idea to hang a chain from his collar and attached a stick to it at its middle, so if he ran, it would bang on his front legs and stop him, or at least slow him down. It worked for about two days, until he figured out that all he had to do was take the stick in his mouth, and then he could run as fast as he wanted without any problem.

Indy's worst bad habit was his love to roam. He just wouldn't stay home; he had that wanderlust and would travel for miles. We had 250 acres, and I'll bet he traveled it all and beyond. I found out from the game warden, Mr. Hast, that he was chasing cattle on a neighbor's farm to the east. The warden told me that if it didn't stop, he would have to be shot. I locked him up, but he always got out, and besides that, he hated not being free.

One day, he didn't come home, so I went out to look for him after school. I knew he was probably over at the neighbor's farm, which, by the way, was about two miles away. I walked over the back ridge and found him lying on an animal path that I had followed to get over there. He had been shot while running away. The bullet had entered around his left hip, traveled through him, and exited through the backbone near his right shoulder. He was still alive but had lost a lot of blood and was near death; his gums and lips were ashen and his eyes dim. I picked him up and carried him home, crying all the way. I couldn't blame the farmer—you can't have dogs running your livestock—but it was hard for me. I put him in the back of the car on an old blanket, and Mom and I drove him to the vet in LaVale. The vet said there wasn't any hope for him, so we brought him home, and he died that evening.

The next day, I buried him in the upper pasture, where he would have plenty of room to run without any fear of being shot. Indy was the last dog brought to the farm while I lived there. You know, death is a familiar visitor to a farm—sometimes it occurs naturally, and sometimes you cause it through butchering or hunting—but when it happens like it did to Indy, it is really hard to accept. Indy was a friend, he was fun, a loyal dog that was always by my side. When he was gone, it left a hollow spot in my heart.

# Chapter 12

# Caring for the Livestock

Having a cattle farm was not an easy undertaking. It was almost impossible to go anywhere for any length of time, as someone always had to be there to tend them—of course, more so in the winter than the summer. But if it wasn't the cattle, it was the chickens or something else. We had four to six milk cattle, depending on the time, and they required daily care. If a cow is giving milk, she has to be milked twice a day; you just can't walk away from her. It was the first thing we did in the morning and then again in the late afternoon. It didn't take too long, but it had to be done. I learned to milk at an early age and would sometimes help milk the cows. We did ours by hand before I went to school. A lot of the kids on my school bus milked before they went to school. It really wasn't a bad job. First, I would get the cow in her stall and give her some grain, then wash the utter and teats with warm water and soap, then rinse them off before milking her into a stainless steel bucket while sitting on a milking stool. I remember in the winter when it was really cold staying as close to the cow as possible and putting the side of my face against her because she was so warm.

Milking before going to school did cause some problems, though. Between having manure on my shoes and leaning against the cow while milking, once the bus got warmed up on a cold morning, I kind of felt like I was back in the barn. That's how it was back then. Most of the kids on the bus were farm kids, and nobody paid too much attention to the odor. Even the bus driver, Harry Bender, never complained.

But back to milking! Once in a while, for reasons unknown, the cow I was milking would kick, and if I didn't have a good grip on the bucket, she would knock it over. After loosing a bucket, I learned how to avoid that problem by pinching the bucket between my legs. Once finished milking, I would take the bucket of milk and pour it into a larger five-gallon milk can and close it off by pressing down on the sleeved-type lid. When all the milking was done, the five-gallon can was taken down to the springhouse just below the barn and placed in the cool water of the spring, which was about two foot deep. There were bricks in the bottom of the spring to set the cans on. By doing this, the milk would cool down quickly and would not spoil. The spring had a good flow, so it continued to cool the milk and held it at a steady temperature, around fifty-five degrees, until the big milk truck came to pick it up, unless we would use it to make butter and cottage cheese.

As I have mentioned before, springs played such an important part in our life at Windale Farms that we couldn't have done without their freshwater supply. It was also a place where natural freshwater critters lived, such as big crayfish, small green frogs, tadpoles in the spring (no pun intended), and small minnows of which I do not know the kind. That springhouse always had phoebes nesting in it during the spring. Their nests were a lot like swallows' nests, made of mud and moss and lined with horsehair. Phoebes had a distinct but easily recognizable call— sounding like *phe-o-be*, with the "phe" being long and the "o-be" quick. Another thing about springs is they are all-natural mineral water and healthy to drink from, and no matter how hot it got in the summer, there was always a place to get a cool drink. The old milk house, which is gone now, had a tin dipper hanging for a refreshing drink.

As I mentioned earlier, we didn't always sell all our milk; we used to keep some for our own use and some to make butter and cottage cheese. Mother had a pasteurizer, a milk separator, and an electric butter churn as well as an egg light in the laundry room. As an aside, the egg light was so Mom and I could candle our eggs for blood spots before we sold them at the store. We used the ones with blood spots at home since there really wasn't anything wrong with them. The separator had two spouts and had to be turned by hand. It was really quite neat. I would pour the pasteurized milk in and then turn the handle; skim milk would come out one spout, and the cream would come out the other. Mother would take the cream and put it in the butter churn, and shortly thereafter, we had butter. Mom would then salt the butter, knead it, form it into pound blocks, and wrap it in waxed paper to be sold at the store. Most of it was promised before it ever arrived at the store; Mom's butter was well sought after.

My grandmother Windish made the cottage cheese. I remember she would pour the milk into a large pan and let it curd up at room temperature, then pour it into cheesecloth sacks and hang it up to drip and dry. Once dry, she would put it in containers and keep it in the refrigerator. It was great cottage cheese. She used to serve it to me after it was just made with a little sugar on it. I'm sure I will never have cottage cheese that is made like that or tastes like that again.

Nothing was ever wasted. Most of the skimmed milk and butter-milk was fed to the hogs, along with the really bad blooded eggs, and the waste produce that dad brought home from the store.

The beginning of life or death of the animals on the farm is a common occurrence. I remember one morning in early spring when Frank, the tenant farmer I spoke of earlier, came up to the house while I was getting ready to go to school to ask for my help. He urged me to come to the lower barn as soon as possible. Man, I thought it was great; I won't have to go to school. Little did I know what I was in for.

One of our heifers had bred too soon and was not able to deliver without help. Frank told me that we would have to lay down the cow so he could tie her and hold her, while I would have to tie leather straps on the front legs of the calf, which were already sticking out, and soap up the birth canal with warm, soapy water. I said, "Are you sure?" He said, "Yes." So I put my hands in the heavily soaped water, shoved them into the birth canal, and lathered the calf's head all around. Then sitting down and putting my feet against the cow's butt and hipbones, I pulled as hard as I could when she would push. I had to soap up her and the calf a few times, and with every push, the calf came out a little farther, until, finally, out came the newborn, into my lap, with all the warm trimmings. Frank told me to quickly cut and tie off the umbilical cord by just making a knot, which I did, and he said the mother would take care of everything else.

The calf was a beautiful white-faced Herford that got up almost as fast as the mother. Wow, was I excited! You would have thought I had just delivered my own firstborn. Frank told me I did well and thanked me for my help. I went up to the house to get cleaned up, and then Mom took me to school and explained to the office why I was late so I wouldn't get in trouble. After that, there was never any doubt what a birth was all about and just what a wonder it is.

# Chapter 13

# The End of an Era

I guess I was about fifteen when Dad decided he had enough of the cattle business. He arranged for an auction to be held at the farm. All the livestock were to be sold, about forty head of beef cattle, including our prize bull Curly, four milk cows, the chickens, and all the equipment, with the exception of what was needed to continue to make hay. It was quite a day. I had never seen anything like it, and all those people, it was just a wonder. I was mostly involved in loading the cattle. We had built a cattle shoot to enable us to load the cattle on trucks using cattle prods. There was a lot of fear in those animals, and it was difficult to get them where we wanted them to go.

I remember one cow that they were having trouble with was about halfway up the ramp when she stopped. Someone punched her with the cattle prod and gave her a good shock, which in turn caused her to fire off a round of hot, runny poop that hit me square in the back and left shoulder. You can imagine there was a lot of laughter from the men around there, including my Dad, but I didn't think it was so funny. I was really embarrassed, but I played along because I didn't want them to think I was a sissy. I had my favorite yellow shirt on too, and that was the end of that shirt.

After the sale, life really changed. There weren't any cattle to tend or chickens to feed or eggs to gather. We didn't need a tenant farmer anymore, so the tenant house stood empty. Most everything I had been accustomed to stopped. Of course, I had grass to cut and stuff to do around the house, but not farm chores. It was difficult for me. Things were kind of solemn without all the activity, and I missed spending time with the tenant farmers, grinding corn, milking cows, and tending the animals.

In the summers that followed, it was my responsibility to make the hay. My job was to mow it down and rake it up with a New Holland side delivery rake that Dad had purchased a few years earlier. I thought that rake was the greatest piece of equipment. When considered against the dump rake, it was like comparing a horse to a tractor. After the hay was cut and raked, I would hire whatever farmer in the area that was available to come in and bale it up. We still had really good hay, especially the timothy and mammoth clover. It was the best hay I've ever seen, and it smelled so good. The mammoth clover is a legume and good for the soil. Like alfalfa, it puts a lot of nitrogen in the soil, which is very prolific, enabling us to get two cuttings a year. Once bailed, the hay was then put in the barn, only now it went into the box stalls and back in the cattle feeding shed stored downstairs so it was easy to sell. In the fall and winter, there were always people coming to get truckloads of hay, and usually by January, it was gone and the barn stood empty again.

Again, I should mention that Dad put me in charge of the hay harvest. I had to determine when it was ready to be cut, watch the weather, cut the hay at a time when it would dry well, then rake it up to be bailed. I had to arrange for the bailing and the help to get it into the barn. I could hire anyone I wanted. If I asked Dad who I should hire, he would say, "Get those that will cause the least amount of work for you and who will do the job right the first time," but he would not tell me who to hire. I knew the guys around the area and which ones would give me a fair day's work. I had to keep their time and pay them, so I got used to having people work for me and being responsible for them. The whole experience was my father's way of teaching me how business worked, how to hire the right people, how to get the job done right the first time, how to be responsible, and how to be respectful to those who assisted me. These are invaluable lessons I have never forgotten, and using them through my entire career has served me well.

I quickly found out that being responsible for the hay harvest sometimes had its challenges. I had to keep everything in working order so it was ready when I needed to use it. I had to be prepared if something were to go wrong, and it always did. I wasn't much of a mechanic, so I had to learn quickly how to recognize when things went wrong and what was needed to fix it.

I remember one time when I hit a tree with the outside wheel of the new New Holland side delivery rake while turning, which resulted in the drive gear for the rake losing a few teeth. I was mortified, thinking I didn't know my life would be that short; surely my dad would kill me when he found out what I had done, or worse, how it had happened. I walked back to the house and told Mom. She understood Dad better than anyone and always took care of me when things didn't go well. Mom understood my predicament and said, "I've got a few dollars put away. Let's go up to the dealer in Frostburg and see if we can buy a replacement gear." Well, Mom and I went to Frostburg and got the part, and she had enough money. I put the gear on the rake and finished raking the hay. It was one of those days that I will always remember but would rather forget.

Mom knew the trouble I had with Dad from time to time; she knew he was pretty hard on me too. However, I suspect she also knew that I would probably be a better person based on what I learned from him, but once in a while, she would come to the rescue and keep me out of hot water. I never knew if Mom ever told Dad about the gear. She probably did, as they were never ones to keep secrets from each other, but if she did, he never said anything to me. Mom and Dad had a great marriage and relationship, and you could tell they loved each other deeply. After all, they had four kids and had built a wonderful life, home, and family together. I always felt very secure with them; nothing in the world would really bother me as long as I could come home to Windale, to Mom and Dad and my family.

# Chapter 14

# The Upper Forty

There was another day when I was clipping pastureland that I would also like to forget. Above the house to the northeast, there was about forty acres of open fields where the timothy and clover grew as well as other open grassland we used for grazing. It was a beautiful summer afternoon but a little unsettled—hot, humid, and still. I was about halfway through clipping the pasture when I looked to the northwest and saw that it was getting pretty dark out that way. In the Evitt's Valley, thunderstorms roll in pretty fast. Keeping an eye on the impending storm, I quickly realized I would not have enough time to get to the barn before the storm hit. In the southeast corner of the upper pasture, we had an equipment lean-to-type shed where we stored equipment over the winter. It wasn't much of a shed but served its purpose well. I decided to quit cutting and pull the tractor and mowing machine into the shed until the storm passed. It was empty at that time, so there was just enough room to get the equipment out of the weather.

Two of the side supports of the shed were trees—one oak and one wild cherry. The other two supports were cut posts. The shed was open on all sides and wasn't very high, so I had to lean over a little to pull into the shed while sitting on the tractor seat. The roof was made of tin and fairly new, so I felt comfortable that I would be dry and safe from the storm. There was a lot of lightning, and it was that cloud-to-ground type that made me a little nervous. Given all that lightning, I decided to stay on the tractor seat to ride out the storm. I should also mention that the mowing machine was attached to the tractor with a three-point hitch and rode on two rubber tires. Its cutter bar was raised up fully, almost touching the roof. I knew that sitting on the tractor seat was the best thing for me to do, given that the lightning was striking everywhere. I felt better knowing that I had rubber between the ground and me. The rain was coming down in sheets, and the wind was blowing the trees around, so I stayed put.

Just about the time I had finished assuring myself that I was safe, a bolt of lightning hit the cherry tree that supported the shed. That lightning strike was one of those that you see, hear, smell, taste, and feel, all at the same time. The cherry tree was about five feet to my left, and all I remember was being totally electrified and seeing a lot of bright lights. My hair stood up, and I couldn't hear or say anything. Plus, I was scared to death that I was going to die, or worse, that I was already dead.

I must have sat there for five minutes or so before coming to my senses. Upon looking up, the first thing I noticed was the smell of ozone and the splintered cherry tree. It was split wide-open in a number of places, with sap boiling out of it, and there were shards of wood all over me and the equipment as well as the rest of the shed. I also noticed water running down my head from a hole in the tin roof that a piece of the cherry tree had made when it fell. It was still raining, so I decided to back up the tractor so I was not under the hole in the roof where the rain was coming in. Can you believe that tractor started just as if nothing had ever happened? When I think about it today, it still amazes me that it started after being electrified. It took a few days for me to feel normal again and to get my hearing back completely, but that sure was an experience I'll never forget.

With the tractor and equipment, it was a good twenty minutes to get to the upper pasture to cut hay, so running back and forth if something went wrong wasn't a viable option. The mowing machine for cutting hay required a lot of maintenance in the field. The pitman rods would break, or the cutter bar teeth would come loose, or a loose tooth would break a cutter bar guard, of which there were many. To get the work done, I had to plan for these things in the field and be prepared to fix them as soon as possible. I devised a toolbox on the back of the tractor that held everything I needed: first the tools needed to do the job, then extra cutter bar teeth and guards; an extra pitman rod; rivets, nuts, and bolts; and a heavy thick piece of steel plate so I would have a place and means to apply the rivets. You know, I still have that same piece of steel plate.

The only other thing I took with me was a big old black glass lined thermos with a screw-on tin cap that was used for a cup. It held about a gallon of cold liquid—in my case, Concord grape juice. We had a Concord grape vine behind the house next to the spring that grew just the best grapes. Each fall, Mom would ask me to gather them, and she would make grape jelly and grape juice. She put the grape juice in mason jars—the kind with the rubber seal that she stretched over the mouth before securing the glass lid with a metal spring clamp—and then put it away for the next summer. It was concentrated, so when

Mom made it for the family, she would add three quarts of cold spring water to one jar of grape juice to make a gallon. In my case, though, when I took the thermos with me to the upper pastures or wherever, Mom would mix the juice with two quarts of water and then fill up the rest of the thermos with ice. On a hot day, there wasn't anything like it, and I never had any left to bring home.

That upper pasture, as we called it, is one of the most beautiful places I have ever seen. It's the highest pastureland on the farm, and its elevation is such that you can see three states at one time—Maryland, Pennsylvania, and West Virginia. You can see both Evitt's and Will's Mountains as well and all the smaller hills in between, all of which run from north to south. Those hills look like large beautiful green humps of emerald all jostling for their place in the valley—just miles and miles of natural beauty. I'm not sure exactly how far you can see, but I know it's well past Cumberland down the Evitt's Valley.

Another unusual feature about this pasture was a spring located at almost the highest point. It always had water in it, and would you believe a few frogs? There was also an old apple tree there that bore apples every year. Of course, the water and apples brought the wildlife on a regular basis all year long. I used to see groundhogs up in that tree quite often. I just loved working up there in that peaceful place, riding along cutting hay or clipping fields, daydreaming and looking at those big puffy white summer clouds slowly floating by. I loved watching the barn swallows swooping around the tractor and catching all those insects I was stirring up with the mower or watching for the rise of a meadowlark or field sparrow in front of me so I could lift the cutter bar to avoid spoiling their nests. To me, life didn't get any better than that. I always felt as though I was a part of all that was around me; I guess I felt like I was part of the spirit of it all, just another creature of nature.

# Chapter 15

# Finding Myself

From the time I was about five or six years of age to around thirteen or fourteen, my physical health wasn't very good. During late fall and through the winter into early spring was the worst time for me. I seemed to catch every bug that came along, especially colds and then bronchitis, which caused a lot of coughing. My sinuses were a big problem—always draining. Sometimes I would hear Mom and Dad talking about my issue, and they always said that the sinus trouble was the cause of everything else. It seemed like every time I turned around, I had an earache. I got the flu almost every winter. All this sickness wore me down to where I was very thin and not very strong. I was different from my sisters and brother. They got sick once in a while but not nearly as much as I did. The earaches were the worst; they always came at night, and I would wake up with this terrible pain.

Mom always came to the rescue and would give me warm eardrops that cut some of the pain. I guess the colds were the next worst problem, with them always settling in my chest. I found out about

Vick's VapoRub at an early age. Mom had bibs made from pieces of flannel that hooked behind my neck with a safety pin. After plastering my chest with Vicks, Mom would apply the flannel, which stuck very well. The Vick's plaster would allow me to breathe the vapors all night, enabling me to sleep better. Mom also used to smear the Vick's under my nose and in my nose, which I really didn't like.

The sad part about all of this was I couldn't do the physical things I saw others do and that I wanted to do, which caused me to question myself and caused sadness. Thinking about it, the constant sickness was only part of the problem that was building in my mind. I lived with three mothers—my mother, her mother, and my dad's mother. They were, of course, all concerned with my well-being and wanted to ensure that I stayed well. I know now that they all meant well, but there was really too much protection: "Don't get your feet wet. Wear your boots. You need an extra sweater on. It's too damp for you to go out and play. It's too cold for you to go out right now. You don't look so good. Are you all right?" My grandmother Stacey, Mom's mother, once told my mother, "Christina, your will never raise that child." Well, you can imagine the confidence that instilled in me. But, to my amazement, I'm still alive and telling you these stories. If you want my opinion, I had the troubles I had due to living with a lot of smokers. My dad smoked a lot of Pall Malls, my grandfather Windish smoked cigars, and my grandmother Windish smoked Old Gold cigarettes; consequently, I was always breathing secondhand smoke.

All of this took a toll on my confidence and self-esteem. I felt that I didn't quite measure up to my peers. My father didn't help much, either. It seemed I never did anything right. There was never praise, mainly criticism. I was convinced for a long time that I didn't have the abilities I needed to fit in or do what was expected of me, which made it hard for me to be socially acceptable, especially in high school—which, by the way, was Fort Hill. I always tried to keep a low profile to avoid being noticed. I looked at myself as a failure and an outcast.

I didn't excel in school and was a pretty bad student. I looked at numbers and didn't see them as they really were. I would read something and would have no idea what I'd read—there was just no comprehension. For example, when I was in fourth grade at Gephart Elementary School, my teacher was Miss Bevans, a real nice lady who treated me well. We had a spelling assignment every day to study for the next day of class, when we would be tested on it. I always studied the spelling list, took the test, and failed. My name was always on the chalkboard in the lower right corner as a person who had to retake the test. I was so embarrassed and ashamed that, at lunchtime, I would sneak back into the classroom and erase my name because I knew I would never pass the test. Miss Bevans never said anything to me. I know she knew what I had done, but I also believe she understood how difficult learning was for me.

After I graduated from high school, Mom and Dad wanted me to go to a local teacher's college in Frostburg, Maryland. We went for the interview with the dean, and as I said, my grades weren't too good from high school. While I was sitting there with them, the dean told my dad that he thought he was wasting his money sending me to college, because I would probably never graduate. That sure instilled a lot of confidence in me! But, you know, college was different. Frostburg was a good school, and the professors cared about me. Some even went out of their way to open my eyes to my potential, and I began to do pretty well. I even made the dean's list a few times, and yes, I did graduate, achieving a bachelor's in education. I got my first paying job teaching school at West Frederick Junior High School in Frederick, Maryland.

I also discovered while I was in college that I was dyslexic, and once I learned how to deal with that, reading and writing became much clearer to me. I have carried those tools I learned and ways to overcome dyslexia with me to this day, knowing that I will always have to try harder and seek help to ensure that I understand things correctly.

The deep feelings and doubts I struggled to overcome in this chapter are mirrored in the following poem.

\* \* \*

## Fences

—*George Windish, October 2008*

*Summer, newly dressed, sings with the sounds of May*
*I travel through rolling fields, damp woods, and ravines*
*Disciplined fences stand as soldiers on guard,*
*Holding prisoner beautiful maidens of clover*
*Morels, as with elves, hide their tripe beneath leaves*
*I alone know their cousins harboring unknown death*

*This solitary day I am free of the critique of others*
*Void of sharp words, questions, eludes of failure*
*A hand coldly sweats against my rifle's blue metal*
*I think of those that would destroy me from within*
*Hearing my friend inside, there is trust, warmth*
*Speaking, "The challenge of confidence demands much"*

*I hold many secrets, their knowledge avoiding shame*
*Their truth holding court dispels unjust and false accusations*

# Finding Myself

Though, not knowing motives cruelly chafes my young soul
Lost pride and uncertainty abound, yoked to this burden
Then fear, my companion always, springs from my mind
My heart pounds with the pain of failing, never knowing

Suddenly I see not what I know before me, trees being strangers
Senses confused, I move timidly with fresh apprehension
Sanctuary lost, the old enemy flows rapidly into my heart
I clearly know him, wrongs, hopelessness, fear, rejection
Searching this unknown place to no avail, my blood is cold
My mind swirls with thoughts and decisions rife with darkness

Twilight is quickly slipping over this strange and unfamiliar terra
Haunting mental blankness brings me long shadows of despair
Turning, circling, brings recent unfamiliar focus to each eye
Using wisdoms secrets, overcome this enemy, challenge him
Don't listen to those that would have you eternally fail
Slowly, depths of uncertainty, throbbing confusion lose their grip

Am I lost in my thoughts, am I lost in my fears, what is lost?
Before me there is an ironwood gate, newly constructed by my hand
Swiftly climbing its jagged wood, I move into flowing fields I
     have treaded
It is now unfenced and beckons me, beckons sweetly with certainty
My body sings with the melody of joy, in concert with my mind
Looking back hopefully in fading light, the ironwood gate
     is gone

# Chapter 16

# My Bedroom

I was never a real social person; being around a lot of people always made me uneasy. I felt that I was inadequate and unable to blend in with large groups, especially with people I didn't know well or at all. Even today, after all these years, I still carry those feelings with me, of which many were reflected in the poem "Fences" from the last chapter. I've never really understood where these feelings came from, but I'm sure that a lot of people find it difficult to understand me, so I have very few close friends, which I find sad. I have some ideas in my mind as to why I am the way I am: one could have been my father, another because I'm dyslexic and had difficulty with comprehension, or maybe it's just something I don't understand. I do know that because of this problem, I passed up many opportunities when I was young because I feared I would fail, when today I know I would not have failed had I tried. I believe I would have overcome much of my problem if I had played sports in high school, but that wasn't to be, because I had to work in the store or work the farm.

The reason I say this about sports is, years later, when I joined the military and had many challenges forced upon me that demanded that I achieve, I realized that I could excel at anything I had to and that there was no need to fear the unknown. The first life-changing decision I ever made by myself was to quit teaching school and join the military in the Army Security Agency. That was the beginning of a whole new way of life for me. I can remember it as clear as if it were yesterday—the night I arrived at Fort Dix, New Jersey, for basic training in early January 1963. I had taken a bus ride from Frederick, Maryland, to Fort Dix, and we arrived late, around eleven at night, and the sergeant herded us off the bus and marched us down a dark street to get our shots. It was a cold, crystal-clear night. I looked up at the stars and felt such a feeling of elation and exhilaration, one like I had never known, and I knew nothing would ever hold me back again—and nothing has.

You are probably wondering what all this has to do with my bedroom. When I was young, before my brother David moved in with me, my bedroom was a place of refuge from all the devils I dealt with. I liked being by myself and in control of what I wanted to do without adult oversight. Keep in mind, though, that I was very much aware of what was expected of me and what pleased those who expected it.

First, let me take a moment to tell you about the room itself. The room was about twenty by twenty feet and had a fireplace with a beautiful mantel and hearth on the east wall. There was an old oversize door with the original hardware on the west wall that opened to the upstairs foyer as well as a door on the north wall that lead to the hallway of my mother and father's bedroom. Two windows faced the south, on the front of the house, one of which opened to the upstairs porch and the other to the outside just to the east of the porch. There was also a small closet in the southwest corner of the room. The floors were hardwood, the ceiling was nine feet tall, and all the walls were made of plaster and covered with wallpaper.

There were two pictures in my room that I must tell you about; they were both about thirty by thirty-six inches in size with large gilded frames. I think both of these pictures were very unusual and not what I would have placed in a young boy's bedroom; nonetheless, they were there.

The first one, which hung over the fireplace, was a black-and-white painting of a very large mother dog, a Saint Bernard type, that was standing on the platform of a very large doghouse to which she was chained by her very large collar, and she and the doghouse were being swept away by a massive flood. Her puppies were all in the rushing water trying to swim to her to no avail and showing great fear in their eyes, especially the one closest to her. The sky was gray and threatening, and the picture illustrated a feeling of great despair and hopelessness. I studied the picture many times but could never understand why that had to be. Oh, I understood what was going on in the picture, but why did it have to happen? What was it telling me about life? Today I know it was telling me that life has great tragedy from time to time with no means to stop it.

The second picture was much less dramatic and in color. It too had a very large dog in it, which looked like an oversized boxer that was a dark-tan color, and again, this one had a very large handsome collar. Being unchained, his stance was one of great strength and discipline while standing guard over an open cradle containing a sleeping baby. Roman architecture framed the setting, with massive half walls, marble floors, and open expanses adorned with beautiful multicolored drapes flowing in a light, gentle breeze. At first glance, all seemed serene and peaceful, giving one the impression that all was well. Then you noticed the ominous, massively large eagle standing on one of the more obscure half walls waiting for his chance to strike and fly off with the new baby. I'm sure I didn't understand this picture very well then, if at all, but later in life, I realized it was the opposite of the first picture, telling me that many tragedies can be avoided with the proper precautions and preparedness.

But enough about the physical surroundings. I loved my room and the warm feeling it gave me. I had my own radio on which I could listen to a number of programs in the evening after dinner. They were usually about fifteen minutes long and ran as a serial, which seemed like they went on forever. My favorite was *I Love a Mystery*. I had a schedule of different shows that I listened to each week. I also had a View-Master that I was fascinated with and a library of "reels" featuring places and animals from all over the world. I could order anyplace in the world and be there when I looked into that wonderful machine. That simple little View-Master brought all of nature right to me. I can still remember some of those pictures to this day, and that must have been sixty years ago. That View-Master was one of my prized possessions.

I didn't read much since it was so difficult for me. I really didn't know why; all I knew was that I just had trouble comprehending written words. I was, however, always a person to keep things in order, and each night before going to bed, I would lay out my clothes to wear the next morning. Everything had its place, and I kept it that way. It was something I could control, something I did myself, and it was always done right.

In the winter, the head of my bed was situated against the north wall of the room, and in the summer, I moved it to the east wall by the window so I could lie there and see the stars and moon. I loved it when the window was open and I could hear all the beautiful nighttime sounds, especially the whip-poor-wills.

Windale had a black cat named Porgy that my grandfather brought home from the store when the cat became ill. We nursed him back to health, and he lived, we guessed, to be twenty-one. He was usually outside at night in the warmer months, and when he wanted to come inside, he would climb the trumpet vine on the west side of the porches, cross the upper porch, jump on the railing, then over to my windowsill, and holler until I let him in through my window. I have always liked cats, and he knew that, so I guess I was an easy touch when it came to getting into the house. Once in, he would just curl up on the bed and go to sleep. I've always had cats and dogs around, and I loved them all. I don't think a man can love completely until he has opened his heart to an animal and received its love in return.

The ensuing poem titled "Follow Me" is a prelude to the next chapter. It explains the profound connection I have with creation. It expresses both joy and fear as well as how I view the creature of the poem as a metaphor for God.

\*   \*   \*

# *Follow me*

*—George Windish, March 2008*

*The summer night is silent and warm*
*My bed feels cool as I lay by the window*
*The hour is late and quiet*
*No one is awake in the old house*

*My mind is only mine and clear of the day*
*I felt as though I could move through the night*
*I looked to the sky and the moon was full*
*I could feel my emotions awaking—I love the night*

*Then, breaking the serenity, He called to me so clear*
*Whip-poor-will, whip-poor-will, whip-poor-will*
*Again and again, He called whip-poor-will, whip-poor-will*
*Announcing that the night belonged to Him and only Him*

*Oh, how I loved this creature of the night, hidden and unseen*
*So near yet invisible to my poor human eye, calling to me so near*
*His sleek body long and of dark colors so close to the earth*
*Again, He called to me, whip-poor-will, whip-poor-will*

*Come with Me if you hear, come to Me if you hear, follow Me*
*Oh, if I could only fly with you tonight, what would I see?*
*If I could leave this earthly prison and soar in the sky*
*My mind was afire with excitement, my body shuddered*

# My Bedroom

If we fly together, old goatsucker, catcher of nights bounty
I will see Your spread wings smooth and without sound
Your whiskers at the ready for Your next catch in Your wide mouth
Your great nocturnal eyes seeing all that is, keeping us safe

You look at me and say, Come with Me, come with Me, let your
    soul be free
I close my eyes and flight comes to me, I too can whip-poor-will
Oh, how my heart is racing and we fly over the farmland I know
    so well
Higher and higher we soar, then diving back nearing the earth

I see my home, white and shining like a pearl in the flood of moonlight
The creek looks like a shimmering ribbon of silver, a crack in
    the earth
And there, yes, there are the cattle and deer grazing in the silver light
I see the white bark of the sycamores with their outstretched arms

Our pond now a giant mirror reflecting our flight to the northeast
We fly over the tallest mountains seeing jagged rocks and gaps
Landing the earth is sweet and cool dew dampens our feet
Whip-poor-will, whip-poor-will, come fly with Me, fly with Me

His flight so sure and true, quickly we move in the cool night air
His sharp eye watching me closely with the surety of time
He says "Look closely and you will see the creatures of the night
They move with silence and stealth, unknowing of our presence"

Now I can hear His thoughts, the thoughts of centuries of knowledge
We have been here forever, flying in the night, together in song

*Watching over the night, feeling its rhapsody, knowing its secrets*
*Our time is ending—we are no longer a part of what is to be*

*Oh no, I cried, without You there will be no night as we know*
*Your song will not ring to introduce the moon and the stars*
*Spring will not be known without Your returning call*
*Your secret will be lost and the earth will cry without You*

*I woke with tears on my cheeks, not knowing of my place*
*My heart was broken and laid heavy in my chest*
*My whole being was confused, hurt, and without understanding*
*I have not heard His call since*

# Chapter 17

# A Passion for Birds

One of the richest pieces of land on the farm was the land that ran along Evitt's Creek and just below the bluff the homestead was built on. All total it was about thirty acres. Its richness came from all the years that the creek flooded in the spring. The flooding deposited rich silt and watered that stretch of land thoroughly each year. The bottomland, as we called it, was used for crops and hay as well as pasture sometimes. The first hay crop usually came in June, and unfortunately, it was the same time the red-winged blackbirds, field sparrows, and meadowlarks were nesting. All three of these birds have distinct calls that were a part of introducing early summer. I couldn't just ignore them and destroy their nests by cutting them down or running over them on the ground. Blackbirds would build their nests in the tall orchard grass and timothy that grew along the creek, which was some of the best hay; the field sparrows and meadowlarks built just about anywhere on the ground. Upon seeing a nest or a bird rise, I would raise the cutter bar on the mowing machine, which gave rise to a patchwork of uncut hay throughout the field, some high and some low. This, of course, didn't sit well with my father, but I knew it was coming and just took the heat. He would tell me to go back and cut the patches down, but I always found reasons not to do it until after the fledglings were out of the nests a few weeks later. Also, since I ran the hay crew, I made sure no one disturbed the nesting places while making hay.

I've always had a fascination for birds. I admire their natural abilities and the way they adapt to their needs. I don't know what brought on this love for these creatures, but our farm was a virtual sanctuary for them. We had quail, chimney swifts, house wrens, redstarts, and whip-poor-wills, just to name a few. Some birds in particular always come to mind—like the barn swallow.

Barn swallows love to nest in buildings, and we had two barns and a number of sheds on the farm that were ideal for them. They could fly through the large openings and land on the many perches in the rafters.

Their nests are largely made of mud pellets mixed with straw and grass and lined with feathers; both the male and female birds spend countless hours building their nests. They would fly and land near water to gather the mud in their beaks, then apply it to the nest. Both of the barns had a run nearby, so there was plenty of mud available. It was apparent where they were getting their mud by the color of the nests, as various types of soil with different colors could be found around the farm. There was always plenty of horsehair or that from a cow's tail for them to line the nest. Once built and dried out, the nest stuck to the perch like glue. It didn't take long for the young to hatch out, and soon the nests would be full of young birds.

Swallows are strictly insect eaters, so they stayed busy until the fledglings were on their own. They are so beautiful and sleek when they fly, with their forked tails, cigar-shaped bodies, and short little legs. Swallows are built for speed and accuracy, enabling them to catch insects on the fly, make tremendous acrobatic turns at will, and dart and change direction in the blink of an eye. When I was mowing, they were a wonder to watch as they flew close to the ground around the tractor, catching insects that I would stir up as I cut. In spite of the fact that there were many flying around me in all directions, there were never any collisions or near misses; their eyesight must be far beyond our abilities as humans. Another thing swallows do that I admire is drinking on the fly. Swooping down and taking a drink from a pond or creek is second nature for them.

Another bird that was at the top of my list is the Baltimore oriole, which has a quickly identifiable song. Back when I was a kid, we had beautiful old elm trees until the Dutch elm disease killed them all. Orioles primarily build their nests in elms; however, they can be found nesting in willow, maple, and apple trees and probably some others as well. Before the blight, there were three grand old elm giants not far from our house—one at each barn and one near the driveway, right by the house. Each of these trees was just enormous, with a spread of about sixty to eighty feet and a similar height, if not higher. There was such majesty about them as they started their spread from a huge trunk into many, many large branches about ten to fifteen feet from the ground, forming a giant canopy. The large branches would arch up and out, then weep toward the ground, becoming thin, wispy ends covered in small pinnate leaves that were so graceful they appeared to dance to the rhythm of the wind when it rustled them.

When the orioles arrived in the spring dressed in their suits of orange and black, the elms were already in full dress, and the days were beginning to get quite warm. After the birds' arrival, they would seek out a place to build their nests on the very end of those wispy elm branches. They would skillfully and firmly attach suspension strings to the branch to form a wrap. Next, they would weave together and actually tie knots of plant fiber, milkweed stalks, strips of gray bark, horsehair, and string or cord to form a gray gourd-shaped structure that was flared at the bottom. A feat of engineering that would be a challenge even for us humans to build. Measuring about six inches deep, the nests had small entrances at the top, and being so well constructed, they were able to withstand the strongest thunderstorm winds they'd encounter. Actually, I have seen these nests survive multiple winters before coming apart and disintegrating. I should also mention that the nests were constructed in such a way and place to be almost indistinguishable with an untrained eye, which afforded the orioles great protection from predators.

Each fall, after the leaves had fallen and the orioles were gone, I would search for one that was hanging close to the ground; usually, they were about thirty feet up. With a well-chosen stick, I would begin the effort of throwing the stick at the thin branch just above the nest to try to break it off, thus releasing the nest. I hate to say how many nests I destroyed, with more throws than I would like to admit, trying to knock one down. But one winter, I got lucky. I waited until the weather was very cold, below freezing; I guess I was getting smarter thinking if I hit the branch when it was frozen, it just might break easier. It worked and down came the perfect nest, completely intact. I was just elated. I had inspected some of the pieces I knocked down but never the whole thing. Finally, I could closely examine the nest firsthand to see and understand what great builders those beautiful birds were. I put it in our heated garage for a while to make sure there weren't any critters in it that might hatch out. Then I took it up to my room and tacked it to the wall just above my bed so I could see it every night before I went to sleep. If I had something special I wanted to hide from whomever, I would to put it in the nest for safekeeping. I was sure no one would ever look in the nest, and as far as I know, they never did. I guess I was about twelve at that time, and that nest was still on my wall when I left for an overseas tour of duty with the military at age twenty-four. It was something I never wanted to part with, but I never saw it again after I left for that tour.

While I was overseas, my father died suddenly, and shortly thereafter, my mother sold the house and farm. I guess no one else saw the value in keeping that old oriole nest, so it probably was thrown away. But, I tell you, if it had been saved, I would still have it hanging somewhere in my home today. That nest stood for a time of passionate curiosity in my life, a time when I learned the value of perseverance and not giving up. In recognizing that God's creations are far more important than those created by the hand of man, I realized for the first time that I was a part of that creation, which made me an important and special part of all things. I realized that I was valuable; I had a purpose just like those orioles in their suits of color that came to visit me every year.

The next poem "Hear The Silence" will take you on a walking tour of the beauty of "Windale's" flora and fauna and terrain.

\*   \*   \*

# Hear The Silence

—*George Windish, July 2008*

*Hear the silence*
*Just before morning, before the sun does rise*
*Just before there's light in sleep-filled eyes*
*The gray mist in the valleys will soon burn away*
*The master cock will soon announce a new day*
*Ducks and geese on ponds will flap and rise*
*Nocturnal ones' quest ending will close their eyes*
*Tomorrow is here with all that it brings*
*How quickly it came as on eagles' wings*

*Hear the silence*
*Of the black nurtured bottomland soil*
*Holding the promise of gifts from ones toil*
*Of June hay rustlings in the warm summer breeze*
*See red-winged blackbirds fly with ease*
*Landing on timothy shafts strong and bold*
*With long seed caps glistening ripe and gold*
*Their nests woven high on grasses strong*
*Not far from the gurgling creek's dancing song*

*Hear the silence*
*Of clear, crisp creek water skipping stone to stone*
*Of a sycamore's touching to show how it's grown*
*Smell freshness in the air as it trips over roots*
*See dragonflies in their bright-colored suits*

*Rolling and flashing in the sun's bright glow*
*Who yesterday were nymphs, dart to and fro*
*Shadows flash below through fast-moving curls*
*Quickly taking their quarry, their tails leaving swirls*

*Hear the silence*
*Of cool springs trickling to form as one*
*They soon find their way as a forest run*
*Providing good water to all that would drink*
*A skunk or rabbit, an occasional mink*
*Bobcat and fox their tracks you will see*
*Armored crayfish and minnows quickly flee*
*Mother Nature's bounty placed solely there*
*Sustaining all creatures, in the sun light fair*

*Hear the silence*
*Of the great forest as it stands true and tall*
*With its majesty and elegance so clear to all*
*Sun canopies shade soft moss below*
*Retaining the moisture from winter snow*
*Soothing rain falls for both young and old*
*Ensuring the promise of red and gold*
*Winter will come stripping leaves to the bare*
*But woodlands will sleep waiting spring without care*

*Hear the silence*
*Of the mountains with their green valley's deep*
*Their streams and rivers promise oceans to keep*
*Having greenbacks of foliage and rocky outcrops*
*Others abandoned and bare with snow on their tops*
*Speak to abundant life and the Earth being young*

*Bring us unbounded beauty with songs to be sung*
*Their commanding silence to the soul quiet brings*
*Their timelessness and stance a part of all things*

*Hear the silence*
*Of the midday heat when the land grows still*
*Of puffy white clouds rising quickly at will*
*West gathering darkness brings a tingle in the air*
*Grazing cattle and horses now moving with care*
*The absence of bird calls from fields and trees*
*Red-eyed cicadas still, as do honey bees*
*Soon the wind moves the trees as waving to God*
*Bring gray sheets of rain to nourish dry sod*

*Hear the silence*
*Of a covey's call as it gathers bobwhite*
*The silence of deer as they forage at night*
*Katydids announce that darkness is near*
*While the call of the nighthawk resounds so clear*
*Cool breezes cease stirring the evening air*
*Bats yawn and flutter quickly from their lair*
*The silence of the night will soon be heard*
*Crickets, stealth owls, and the whip-poor-will bird*

Mother and Dad had friends by the name of Ed and Helen Vandergrift. Ed was a contractor who had built a beautiful country estate not too far from our home. Ed was probably my father's best friend. He and Helen visited our home quite often, and all of us kids got to know them very well. They had a big swimming pool at their house, and we would get invited to go over to their home often, which was a real treat. As a matter of fact, we knew them so well that we called them Aunt Helen and Uncle Ed. Aunt Helen knew that I loved birds, and one year, on my birthday, she gave me an Audubon bird book, which contained all the information I could ever want to know about all the birds in North America. What a wonderful gift! I had taught myself about birds up to that point, learning their names, songs, and such, but I really didn't know much about them. This book changed all that; I could now actually do research and read about them and understand so much more. This book not only had descriptions about each bird, but also details about what they ate, where they could be found, what their nests looked like and how they were constructed, the way their songs sounded, and their migration routes—the book was just a wonder. Well, shortly after Aunt Helen gave me the Audubon book, my mother bought me a field guide with sighting charts. That was all the incentive I needed to get out and explore! It was June, so all the birds were back. I spent the rest of the summer in discovery, bird-watching and recording sightings. By the way, I still have that Audubon bird book in my library.

*Me getting ready to go to bird camp*

The following summer after school was let out, Mom and Dad made arrangements for me to attend bird camp through Gephardt Elementary School, where I attended. The camp was located in Garrett County, which is the most western county in Maryland and is bordered by Pennsylvania to the north and West Virginia to the west and south. Elevation-wise, Garrett County is up there. I had to travel up the Allegany front, which is west of Cumberland, to get there. Bird camp was held at the Boy Scout camp, and it was one of the most beautiful places I had ever seen. Located on a lake, there were alpine meadows, bogs, and old forest—much I had never seen before. In addition to the dining hall, there were rustic wooden cabins and outdoor classrooms. All this was just a whole new world for me. Two of my classmates from grammar school—Bill Spoerl and Bill Brown—were there as well, which made me feel more comfortable since I had never been anywhere without my mother or father, or even my older sister Christina. But there was a lot of anxiety on my part, and each night, it manifested itself in my wetting the bed. If that wasn't bad enough, my bedroll consisted of a large red-and-black woolen blanket. Well, you guessed it, the red dye in the blanket ran on everything—me, the mattress, and anything in its wake. I was so embarrassed, especially when I had to put my mattress and blanket outside to dry in the sun each day. But all that aside, I had a great experience. I saw an oven bird for the first time as well as a Venus flytrap catch and dissolve a fly, swam in the lake, and realized just how much nature there was for me to discover and explore.

There is something about bird-watching that becomes a passion. There seems to be such great satisfaction in seeing a bird for the first time and discovering its identity. Once you get hooked, no matter how old you are or where your life has taken you, that passion never leaves you. Two summers ago, I discovered a new species I had never seen before on my farm in South Carolina—a Louisiana water thrush! It was still a thrill even sixty years after receiving that Audubon bird book and first experiencing the passion. Also, last summer, I saw a woodcock on my property. I haven't seen one of those since I left Windale, but I knew what it was immediately. Woodcocks are basically sandpipers that left the ocean and never returned. They are great game birds, one of many that were part of the old homestead.

We had many coveys of quail, and there is nothing sweeter than hearing their bobwhite call in the morning to introduce the day or their urgent call to gather the covey to rest late in the evening. Turkeys and pheasants were few and far between then, but we had a number of ruffed grouse. They are absolutely beautiful birds that, upon lifting off, could turn your hair white with fright and befuddle your ability to lift your shotgun to fire, let alone fire it with accuracy, to say nothing about almost stopping your heart. They fly with ease through heavy woods at great speeds yet never hit anything and just vanish.

Before I conclude my discussion of birds, I must tell you about whip-poor-wills. Whip-poor-wills are part of the family of night-flying birds called nightjars that include nighthawks and chuck-will's-widow. I'm sure you have heard their call—if not firsthand at night, then certainly in the movies or on television as a background bird call. But they are always portrayed calling during the day, which, of course, they never do. There's nothing more mystifying than hearing their call off in the distance on a dark summer night, and conversely, if they call close to you in the middle of the night, they will wake you with a start because of how loud they are, especially if they stay and repeat their call over and over and over again. There is an old legend that the only way you can stop them from staying and calling over and over again is to turn your shoes upside down under your bed. I never tried it, so I don't know if it works. All kidding aside, they are wonderful, magical birds that few of us ever get to see.

Living as I did in the country afforded me so much freedom. Even being young, I was able to wander all over our farm without worry; my parents gave me a lot of latitude to explore and learn about the nature I loved so much. I thank God for that time in my life. Most, if not all, of what I learned while living at Windale has stayed with me, stayed clear in my mind, and has impacted much of what I am today.

# Chapter 18

# Hunting

I never thought about hunting very much when I was young. My grandfather used to go hunting; I assumed that because he had a shotgun. I'm not sure of the make anymore, but I do remember it was a twelve-gauge double-barreled shotgun with a leather boot on the stock that laced up like a shoe. My father's brother, George, and his son, Albert, or Al, or Albee, as we all called him, were both hunters—mainly of rabbits. They would come on occasion to visit and always came in the fall so they could rabbit hunt. I'm quite sure that Grandpop's shotgun wound up with them somewhere along the line because I didn't see it around in later years.

Just as an aside, Al was the only cousin I had; Uncle George and Aunt Betty had just the one child, and my father did not have any other brothers or sisters. My mother, Christina Anna Louise, was an only child. All of this made for a very small family. I'm sure you noticed that I was named after my father's brother, and Al, my cousin, was named after my father.

Back to hunting! Sometimes I would go hunting with Uncle George and Al, but I didn't have a gun. I learned a lot about hunting from them, especially how to work hunting dogs. As I remember, they always brought a dog, a beagle type, to hunt rabbits. I learned that rabbits, once jumped by the dog or the hunter, would tend to run in large circles, so you could anticipate about where they would show up again. The dog was well trained and would bay with his deep-toned bark as he ran the rabbit, bringing it around for the shot. They always hunted on what we called the pine fields just up the hill to the southeast of the house. The pines were very young, with a lot of grasses, tall weeds, and raspberry brambles—just a great place for rabbits, similar to the place that Uncle Remus described. We could always count on jumping as many rabbits as we wished. The pine field, by the same token, was a difficult place to hunt due to the thickness of the growth, which made it hard to get a clear shot, but I guess that leveled the playing field somewhat for the rabbits. We had to know what we were doing to bag a few rabbits there.

Those experiences I had hunting with my uncle and cousin kindled an interest for hunting in me that grew as I did. I guess I was about twelve when I decided I wanted to own a gun. There was just one problem—my father. He wasn't a hunter, didn't want to hunt, and didn't want me to have a gun or be out in the woods hunting. However, if there's one thing about me that I have always been, it's tenacious. Once I made up my mind, I knew, one way or another, I was going to have my own gun.

Charlie O'Neal, a good friend of mine whose nickname was "Carty," lived about a mile or so from me in a hollow just off Hazen Road—and Carty's father had a gun for sale. I used to get together with Carty sometimes on Saturdays or during the summer when we were off from school. He was a great guy, and I see him if I can when I visit Cumberland. He looks and sounds the same as he did then, just sixty years older. He still has that same spark about him and is a great storyteller, but what I notice the most is he still has that same twinkle in his eye as he did back then. Anyway, the gun he had for sale, which was five dollars, was pretty old and hadn't been used for a long time. It was a twenty-five-caliber rim fire single-shot with a rifled octagon barrel; the stock was beat up pretty badly, and the bluing was mostly gone. To me, though, it was the best gun in the world, and I wanted it. However, dad didn't think it was a good idea for me to have a gun, and I didn't have any money to buy it on my own.

When I started high school, I used to get an allowance of three dollars a week that I had to use for lunch money at school. The least expensive lunch cost me thirty-five cents a day, which added up to $1.75 a week, and I wasn't one to miss lunch, so the rest was for me to use as I saw fit. I sometimes went to a movie in town or something like that and used some of it, but for the most part, I saved it in a little old wooden bank that I kept on my dresser in my bedroom so I would have money when I went to my grandmother Stacey's house at the beach each summer. The bank could be locked with a small brass key, which I hid away in different places in my room from time to time; one of those places was that oriole's nest I spoke of earlier. Upon checking my bank, I discovered I did in fact have enough money. If I waited until the next week and skipped a few lunches, I could buy the gun and did so the first opportunity I had to visit Charlie.

Once purchased, I set out to redo the stock. I had never done anything like that before, so I just started sanding it by hand, which didn't work very well due to it being in such bad shape. I began looking for another way to get the job done. We didn't have anything around like a sander, but I did, however, find an old electric motor in the garage that still worked. I wrapped sandpaper around the drive shaft of the motor, which was about four inches long, and left enough of it unwrapped as to form a flap-type arrangement, and it worked just fine to sand down that stock. Bluing was a different story. I had no idea how to re-blue a gun barrel, so I went down to a hobby shop in Cumberland that was across Henry Street from Stacey's Market. The owner explained to me how it worked, and I bought a kit, followed the directions, and voila, the gun looked like new.

There was just one more problem—the gun had no firing pin. Because of the gun's age, I didn't have a clue where to buy a firing pin for it, thus I improvised and experimented by using finishing nails I found in the barn. The first one I fashioned was too short, so the gun wouldn't fire, and the second was too long, so when it fired, it blew back by the hammer, which was very dangerous and could have blinded me. Well, I finely got it the right length, and the gun fired great—with one exception. If I pointed the gun too high, the pin would fall out. To overcome this problem, I carried a stash of pins in my coat pocket.

I did a lot of target practice to improve my accuracy so I would be ready when hunting season opened. The first season to open was for squirrel. Squirrel season opened every year on October 5, unless that day was a Sunday, and then it opened the following day. Each year, starting in September, squirrel season was the topic of discussion on the school bus. All the kids who were squirrel hunters started what they called "spotting squirrels" prior to the season. The process, usually done after school or on the weekend, included checking out past squirrel-hunting areas to see if they were still good places to hunt or looking for new locations. When spotting, one would look for nut cuttings, squirrels nests, and any other signs of their presence. Now that I had a gun and was prepared for my first season, I paid attention and asked a lot of questions about this process so I too could do my own squirrel spotting. I found out quickly that you never—and I mean *never*—disclose your hunting areas to anyone, not even your best friend. From what I had learned, though, I was able to determine that there were a number of areas I knew that might be good habitats for squirrels. I could find squirrels in most of the wooded areas of the farm, but the best places for them were along the edges of the fields, where the oaks, hickory, walnut, and other trees squirrels preferred were clustered. Like anything else, the more I hunted, the more I learned about the best ways to be successful.

I remember very clearly, just like it was yesterday, the first day I went squirrel hunting. I wasn't able to go the morning of the first day of the season because it was a school day, and with Dad, there was no skipping school. But that afternoon, I was able to go. I may as well have stayed home from school that day since I couldn't think of anything else anyway. I was totally preoccupied with getting home and going up on the hill to the top forty acres where I had spotted squirrels many times and knew there was a good chance I would get one. Well, I finally got to my spot and quietly waited and waited. I guess I thought the squirrels were going to wait for me to get there and then come out to do their thing.

Not too far from me, I thought I heard some nut cuttings falling from a hickory tree. I crept very slowly toward the sound; it stopped, so I waited, and then it started again. Ever so slowly and with great care, I got close enough to see the squirrel near the top of the tree, but there wasn't a clear shot and I didn't want to miss my first chance. I tried to get closer, but he heard me and ran to the main trunk of the tree and hid on the other side. What to do? I sat down and waited, and finally, he began moving again. I had gotten pretty close to the tree when he showed himself. I raised my rifle high and sighted—a clear shot.

The main problem I had was controlling my breathing. I felt like I had just run a mile uphill, and now I was trying to remain still and hold my breath in order to get a good shot. I learned later that I had buck fever. I don't know where it comes from, probably something primeval, but you sure can't control it when it happens. Then, to make things worse, just as I pulled the trigger to fire, with the end of my barrel swirling around from the buck fever, the firing pin dropped out of my rifle onto the ground. Of course, when I reached in my pocket for another pin, I was spotted again by the squirrel. Off the squirrel went from tree to tree toward the creek—he was long gone.

I quickly learned with that experience that if I were going to get a squirrel with that rifle, I would have to be farther away so I wouldn't have to lift the barrel so high that the firing pin would drop out. I would have to be a pretty good shot to hit a squirrel with a single-shot rifle to start with, and the farther away I got from it just compounded the difficulty. I was angry with myself, angry at the rifle, and it was starting to get dark, so I retreated back to the house.

Dinner was on the table when I got home, so I got cleaned up and sat down. I guess I looked kind of dejected, because everyone wanted to know what had happened. I just told them I didn't see anything and let it go at that; I was too embarrassed to tell the story. Besides that, Dad didn't know about the rifle and wasn't happy with the fact that I was hunting to start with.

Well, the next day, Dad was home when I got home from school. He never left the store early, and I didn't understand why he was home. He told me he intended to go hunting with me to ensure nothing went wrong. That's just what I wanted—for my friends to find out I couldn't go hunting unless my daddy was with me. Besides that, he didn't know anything about hunting. For all I knew, he had never been hunting for anything. But I wanted to go, so I did what I had to do. I didn't want to take him to the places I had spotted—I'm not sure why, I just didn't. I took him up the hill to the right of the barn where I knew there were some large oaks, then loaded the rifle and sat on a log with him and waited. Dad was a smoker, and it wasn't long before he had to have a cigarette. Great, I thought, we wouldn't see any squirrels now for sure.

Just about that time, one came moving through the trees to where we were. Forgetting Dad was even there, I positioned myself so I could get a shot, raised the barrel, pulled the trigger, and fired. I missed that squirrel by so much Dad probably figured he didn't have to worry about me. I reloaded and aimed for another shot, and you guessed it, the firing pin fell out. Man, I was so angry and embarrassed. I reached into my pocket, got another pin, and put it in position, but the squirrel wasn't a fool—he was off for safer surroundings. Dad looked at me and said, "What happened?" So I had to tell him the whole story, and then he said, "No more hunting with that rifle until you get it fixed!" I was crushed, but I knew he was right, so we trudged back to the house.

The next day, on the bus and at school, all my classmates were talking about their hunting successes. I was really down in the dumps. When I got home from school, it was a beautiful day, just perfect to go hunting, but not for me. As I walked in the lane to the house, I spotted Dad's car. I couldn't believe that he was home again; like I said, he never left the store early. Well, I came into the house and asked Mom why Dad was home, and she said he wanted to see me in the dining room. I walked into the dining room, and Dad was sitting at the head of the table where he always sat. I couldn't believe what I saw next.

In the middle of the table, there was a brand-new twenty-gauge Remington pump shotgun and a box of number six shells. My dad had bought me a brand-new shotgun! When I think of it as I am writing this story, I get that same feeling I had way back then. I remember my throat getting tight, wanting to cry, and feeling amazed. He had done it for *me*. This man who never told me that I did anything right, the one who complained about me all the time, the one I had always believed didn't really care for me that much, he had bought *me*—yes, *me*—a new shotgun.

What a wonderful discovery I made that day because of his gift. It was clear my father loved me and cared about me and wanted me to be safe. He didn't want his firstborn son to be ashamed of himself or his father, but most of all, I realized he had confidence that, even at a young age, I could handle responsibility and be someone whom he could trust and be proud of. I learned that you cannot judge by inaction, only actions taken. I will never forget that day. I didn't have many like it with my father in his short lifetime, but that day, he was a shining star, my shining star. For me, that day was the beginning of understanding Dad better.

Hunting became important to me for quite a few years after that—I guess until I started college. Some things stand out in my mind about those years. I remember one time when I went hunting after school on a beautiful fall day—one of those days when it's about eighty degrees with no wind and the leaves are a rainbow of colors. It was quite dry in the woods, so every move was noisy. The only thing to do was to find a comfortable spot and sit down against a tree and wait. I went to the upper pasture and settled in at one of my favorite spots. The next thing

I remember was waking up in the dark. I had never walked down from the hill in the dark before, and it's amazing how different things are at night. When I got home, everyone was concerned and about to come looking for me. Mom said she had rung the big bell many times, but of course, I didn't hear it, as I was asleep.

Another time, I was sitting next to a tree when a squirrel scurried down the trunk above me. I sat very still, waiting for my opportunity. Then all of a sudden, *bang*! Some unidentified hunter had shot the squirrel about ten feet above my head, and it fell to the ground in front of me. I was so shocked that I just sat there—I guess afraid to move. Then this unknown guy stood up and started walking toward me. When he saw me, he turned around and took off running down the ravine and disappeared. That's the only near miss I ever had when hunting. I never did tell my mom or dad about the incident; some things are better untold.

I guess by now you have figured out that squirrel was my favorite game to hunt. There was just one problem—the only people in our family who liked to eat squirrel besides me were my grandmother and grandfather Windish. Grandmom used to stew them, and I always liked stew of any kind. When I was young, I just didn't like meat, and stew was one way I would eat it. I enjoyed putting a pile of stew on a piece of bread—now, that was good! The problem I had with hunting squirrels was I got more squirrels than we could eat at home.

I didn't like to kill things if they weren't eaten. I was never one to kill something just for the sport of it. I remember one time I did, though. Using my .22, I shot a buzzard that was circling overhead just to see if I could hit it. It was way up, so I really didn't think I had hit it, but I did and down it came. I was really sorry that I had, but there it was—big, dead, and stinky! I picked it up by the foot, took it to the barn, and hung it upside down from one of the rafters—I'm not sure why, I guess I wanted to show it to Norney or somebody. Well, I forgot about it until about a week later, and when I went to the barn—mind you it was summertime—that old buzzard really reeked, so I cut him down and buried him behind the barn.

Now, back to shooting more squirrels than we could eat, I'm not sure how this came about, probably through my grandfather, but the lady who ran the cigar store at the corner of Fredrick and Center Streets in downtown Cumberland came into my dad's market and said she loved squirrel and would pay me for all those I brought to her. What a deal—no more worries and I charged her twenty-five cents a dressed squirrel, which gave me plenty of money for shotgun shells and some left over for the bank.

I used to hunt other game like quail, woodcock, or sometimes rabbits, but not too often. I never hunted deer; I just had no desire to do it. I used to go coon hunting with the game warden, Mr. Hast, but I never carried a gun. Coon hunting is a rather crazy sport. We would take the dogs out into the woods at night, then turn them loose, and when they picked up the scent of a coon, they would take off after it. We had to run after them until they got the coon treed, and it never ceased to amaze me how those crazy dogs would try to climb up to that treed coon. Sometimes, if there were low limbs on the tree, the dogs would get ten or fifteen feet up the tree. After the coon was treed, someone was appointed to shoot the coon in such a way as to not destroy the value of the pelt. Once the coon was killed, all the dogs were given an opportunity to get a good whiff of it, and then it was placed in a burlap sack, which I sometimes carried home. Mr. Hast always had lot of coon pelts tacked up on his barn to cure.

I remember hunting one night up near Lake Gordon when the hunters lost two dogs. This happened because the coons, once their scent was picked up, would run to the lake and swim out a ways, and when the dogs came in after them, the coons would climb on the dogs' backs and drown them. Coons were very smart in many ways. I guess I would have to say the most I ever got out of coon hunting was a lot of scratches and scrapes from running through the woods at night. It wasn't really my favorite sport—nope, not at all!

For two years, Norney and I ran a trap line along Evitt's Creek in the wintertime. Once we learned the signs, it was easy to find out where the muskrats were, and there were quite a few. We set out about sixty-some traps, most of which were water traps. Water traps would drown the animal when it got caught. We sold our skins to Sears Roebuck out in St. Louis and made enough money to make it worthwhile, but it was hard getting up in the morning and checking the traps before school. Switching off each day made it better, though. On weekends, we would check them together. Then, late one winter, we lost all our traps in a flood, and that ended the trapping. It was probably just as well. I'm not sure I cared too much for trapping; I think it was more Norney's idea, and I liked him, so I went along with it. It was an experience, however, that taught me a lot about things I never would have learned any other way.

One story I must tell you about trapping, before I get off the subject, is my adventure with trapping foxes. By the way, I never did catch one, but I learned from a book I had just how to do it. Foxes are very smart and wary of anything unusual. I had to smoke the traps along with my boots and gloves to avoid leaving a scent at the trapping areas that I set up. I used to hang pieces of chicken above a triangle of traps that were set below, then camouflage the traps as best I could. One problem I had was my dog Indy. He always came along and probably left enough scent for both of us, but there was no going without him, and I guess I really didn't care. I used to set the traps up the ravine behind the barn in places I thought were best.

One day after school, I went up to check the sets. I checked the first set—nothing. I checked the second set—nothing. Finally, I checked the third set—a skunk! It wasn't very happy being trapped. Indy got very excited, and I knew I had a problem! The skunk squirted Indy in the face, and Indy started to howl and rub his face on the ground. I knew I had to get that skunk out of the trap, but how? I always carried a pistol with me and a large smooth wooden club so I could hit the game in the head without damaging the pelt prior to removing it from the trap. The skunk, however, was caught by two traps. I didn't want to shoot it, so I moved in with the wooden club and took a swing. Before I could make contact, the skunk hit me first with his "eau de skunk" square on my right cheek. The stench was really bad—and I mean *really* bad. It was all I could do to keep from throwing up. After that, I shot the skunk, and Indy and I headed home.

When I got home, I told Mom what happened, but I think she knew before I told her. She made me take off all my clothes and wash in a pan outside on the back porch, where it was very cold out there. I smelled so bad that I didn't go to school for two days, and I'm sure the whole family would have liked it if I had found another place to live for a while. My grandfather thought it was all very funny. When I finally did go to school, I took a bottle of Old Spice shaving lotion with me to try to cover up the stink, but it really didn't work too well. I was so embarrassed! God, I wish I could have crawled in a hole for a while and disappeared.

# Chapter 19

# Fishing

April 15 was another important date on my calendar; it was the first day of trout season each year. Evitt's Creek was a trout stream—or I should say, used to be a trout stream. Long before I started fishing, the native trout had disappeared from Evitt's, so the state would stock it with rainbow trout prior to the start of the season. There was always a lot of speculation as to where and when it would be stocked. I guess if I'd known where they dumped in the fish, I probably would have had a better chance of catching my limit. Evitt's Creek ran about two miles or so along our property line, which really didn't give me any advantage, because the state usually stocked the trout at the two road bridges—one below our house across the bottom field and the other down Mason Road at the big swimming hole. There was also a bridge that crossed Rocky Gap Creek just before getting to the swimming hole. The state probably stocked at that bridge too. Interestingly enough, Rocky Gap still had some small native brown trout, but very few. My friends Nelson and Steve Robison probably had the best advantage when the season opened, as they lived next to the old schoolhouse, which was right beside the Rocky Gap bridge and only a good stone's throw from the swimming hole. On the first day the season opened, all they had to do was walk right outside their door and they were right there at two of the three prime spots.

Like squirrel season, there was a lot of preparation necessary to be ready for the first day. Worms, you had to have worms. They were by far the most important item. Gardens were a favorite place to dig for them. Once dug, they were transferred to a worm bed. When needed, plenty could be dug up from the bed and then transferred into a worm box, which hooked to your belt for easy access. Manure was also a good place to find a substantial stash of worms. I didn't have a garden to dig in, but we sure had plenty of manure, and that was usually where I got them. One of my best friends Bill Spoerl, whom I had known since grammar school, lived in town on Bedford Road. Bill was an avid trout fisherman. This guy lived for fishing. Bill always called and asked if he could come out to my house and stay overnight so he could be at the creek at the crack of dawn to start fishing. Every year, we did a lot of planning to get ourselves ready. For example, we would go out to the Cumberland Country Club's golf course at night to gather night crawlers. Night crawlers were the biggest and best worms for trout fishing. If you had the genuine article, there was no doubt that you would catch fish; at least we believed it, so it must have been true.

On the first day of trout season, it was a madhouse near the bridges; men and boys would come from all over to fish. Some fished from the banks or in the stream wearing hip boots, while others fished off the bridges. The fish never had a chance; to them, it was like feeding time at the hatchery. I think if you threw in a bare hook, they would hit it. It was kind of silly, if you think about it; there wasn't a whole lot of sport to it. In a few days, the fish were all gone, and only a few diehards went fishing after that. Then the rumors would start all over about the second stocking, and so it went.

# Chapter 20

# The Farm Pond

Back in the late 1940s and early 1950s, the federal government had a program to assist in the conservation of water resources. If you owned a farm and had a logical reason to build a pond, it was a safe bet that the government would assist you in getting it done. This is probably another activity Dad learned from reading the *Gentleman Farmer* magazine. Dad decided to build a pond just north of the house on the bottomland, where there were springs and swampy land. The pond was also designed to catch the runoff from the upper forty acres on the hill to the east. It worked so well that the first spring after the pond was built, it filled up completely. Dad decided to stock it with fish—bass and bluegills. Not too many springs passed before it was a lot better fishing than Evitt's Creek; plus, I didn't have a season, or have to fight for a place on the bank, or need a license.

There were some problems, though, from time to time. One year, the muskrats from the creek decided to take up residence in the pond. If we were not careful, they would drain our pond by digging into the banks and causing it to seep or leak. We—or I should say, I—had to trap and get rid of them. Another problem was snapping turtles. Anytime there are fish in a pond, there are also snapping turtles. They can get pretty big and consume a lot of fish. The best way to control them is to fish them out.

My grandfather was well versed in fishing for snappers; he taught me just what to do. First, I started out with a heavy wire that would span the width of the pond. Next, I hung wire leaders with good-size hooks at the end from the wire and then hooked chicken heads or parts from the hook. Finally, I stretched out the wire over the pond by hooking it to a post, tree, or something on either side and left it overnight.

The first day, we had four big snappers out of a total of seven hooks. That was the easy part. The turtles may have been hooked, but they are really mean and nasty critters that are out to win. They are one of the ugliest animals I have ever seen and are not to be messed with. No matter what needs to be done with them, it needs to be done right and fast. First thing I did was haul them up on the bank over a large board and quickly chop off their heads with a hatchet. Grandpop told me he once saw a snapper bite a stick in two even after its head had been severed from the body. Needless to say, I left the heads alone for a few days before taking them off the hooks. The positive side of all this was we were able to keep them under control, but it was impossible to completely get rid of them. Also, Grandpop showed me how to clean them and get the meat out. Once the meat was removed, Dad sold it at the store. He always had a call for all we could catch.

That pond had a lot of other positive things about it other than conservation. We could ice-skate on it in the winter, and we could swim in it in the summer. I built a raft so we could float around the pond, and there was always good fishing. We kept geese named Hansel and Gretel, which, by the way, thought they owned the pond and were very protective of it. I quickly found out it wasn't wise to turn my back on either of them. We also had mallard ducks with clipped wings, which could still fly, but not for any significant distance. The pond was always full of frogs—green frogs, bullfrogs, and many peeper frogs. The peepers were the first frogs heard in the spring of the year. Bats and barn swallows would drink from the pond on the fly, and when the cattle were at pasture on the bottomland, it was their water source too. Finally, if there was ever a fire at the house, the fire company would have used it for water.

I visited the farm last year (2010), and the pond was still there and just as healthy as it was sixty years ago. I did notice, though, that there were blue herons visiting the pond, which we didn't have back when I lived there, as well as Canadian geese using it for nesting and a resting spot in the late afternoon and evenings when on their way to a beautiful lake at Rocky Gap State Park. It still had fish and turtles and was still serving the water conservation it was intended for. One other thing that should be mentioned is even during the driest times it always had plenty of clear, clean water because it is spring fed.

There was something peaceful about that pond—the kind of peacefulness felt when all is well. On warm spring and summer evenings, I remember slipping down to the pond and sitting on the bank, sometimes the east bank and other times the west bank, and just taking it all in. Sitting on the east bank, I could watch the sun set; sitting on the west, I could see night fall. It was kind of mesmerizing, like sitting in front of a fire and staring at the flames. I would sit there and realize just how wonderful my life was. It was a great place to sit and dream about what was to come. I used to think about things like what kind of work I would do, whom I would marry, where I would go to college, how many children I would have, and what God had in store for me. I've always known that God had a place for me and a job for me to do, so when things didn't go the way I'd expected, all I had to do was wait and he would provide me with the new direction I needed.

While sitting there, I was alone with my thoughts, and there wasn't any reason to be afraid of life. As the sun went down at my back, the chimney swifts would begin circling the old house, all flying clockwise, preparing to drop into one of the many chimneys where they would spend the night. The fish were still jumping to grab an insect or two before dark. There were turtles floating with only their heads above water, showing no sign of movement. Then, as darkness started to fall, I could feel the brisk air envelop my shoulders. The first bats would start to leave their roosting places in the old house. Some roosted under the spouts, others under the terra-cotta tiles along the outermost edges of the east and west walls, while still others came out of the portico, among other places. The first thing they did after a circle of the house was head down to the pond for a drink on the fly, and then it was off on the night's hunt. Soon the bullfrogs would begin their deep-throated croaks to be joined by other smaller frogs. All of a sudden, I would realize that there were many different insect sounds all around me, each calling to another, all distinct, and all driven to mate and continue their kind. I especially liked the katydids, scratching out their rhythmic sounds on their thorax, as did their cousins the crickets. By this time, the first stars were twinkling in the sky, along with the solid glow of the planets. The one I most enjoyed was the evening star, Venus, which would set just after the sun, depending on the time of the year. I always stayed a little longer before going up to the house, waiting for the first call of a whip-poor-will, my favorite night sound of all and one of my most favored birds. Such a wonderful peace was to be found ending the day on the bank of that pond.

# Chapter 21

# The Old Millrace

I mentioned before that the pond was built mainly to conserve both soil and water. Its location was ideal for catching the runoff from the upper forty acres because it was situated near an old millrace. If you remember, in one of the earlier chapters, I explained that the founder of the farm, Henry Smouse, built a gristmill as the primary means of supporting his homestead. You may find it hard to believe, but when we moved there, that old millrace was still in pretty good shape—one hundred plus years after it was built. Of course, it didn't have water in it anymore. The race was a natural catch basin for all the runoff water from the upper fields; all we had to do was modify the berm by cutting drains into it, which would gradually let the water run into the pond. Every year, in the late winter or early spring when the snow started to melt or when the first heavy rains came, I remember having to put on my buckle-down galoshes and going down to the race to clean out the leaves and debris from the cuts so the water would drain into the pond. The pond had a long finger to the north, which looked like a large appendix running parallel to the race that was about ten feet wide and maybe seventy-five yards long. It provided for about six or eight drains in the race that fed into the pond. Opening up those drains was a cold, wet job. This may sound strange, but I looked forward to doing that job every year; it was like a tradition, something I was supposed to do, a good feeling, a feeling of being part of the new season that was coming.

I'm sure that millrace was distinctive, even in its day, due to being a mile or more long. The length was necessary to get the proper fall of water at the speed and volume necessary to run the mill. From the race head, beginning on Evitt's Creek and continuing all the way to where the homestead stood, it ran along a sharp bluff about two hundred feet high. It was obviously hand dug from a heavy shale-type soil, and the tailings from the dig were used to build the west berm. The race width was about eight to ten feet across at its top and five to six feet at the bottom. Depending where it was dug, it ranged from four to six feet deep. Over the years, it has filled in with some leaves and eroded shale, but for the most part, it looks quite a bit like it did back then. As you would suspect, it generally follows the same direction of the creek. Because of this, the floodplain of the creek comes right up to the berm in some places as well as to the foot of the bluff. It is very unique in its construction—designed to maintain the fall of water on a consistent basis.

The race location made it difficult to get to; thus, for the most part, it has been protected all these years from any kind of development, farming, or logging. That protection for over 170 years allowed old-growth timber to cultivate on and around the race, the bluff, the berm, and the floodplain. The most unique trees are found on the berm, and the biggest are sycamore, black walnut, and sugar maple. The sycamores, sometimes called the sequoias of the East, were and still are some of the biggest I have ever seen—just magnificent trees. To me, the plentiful sugar maples were—and again, still are—the most intriguing.

Once I realized that maple syrup comes from sugar maple trees, there was no stopping me! I wanted to make maple syrup. I studied and learned all I could, and one late winter's day when I knew the sap had started running, I tapped my first trees with a carpenter's hand drill, plugged the holes with hollowed bamboo, and then hung buckets just below the tap. It wasn't the best arrangement, but it was so exciting to see the first sap run into those buckets. It took a long time—a lot longer than I'd anticipated—but I finally got what I thought was enough to begin cooking it down.

Mom was a great supporter and worked with me through the cooking-down process. Neither one of us knew much about what we were doing, but we did make a batch of about a pint of syrup that year. It wasn't anything like the fine amber color bought in the store. As a matter of fact, it was quite dark, but despite that, it tasted really good, and everyone—I guess everyone because no one ever complained about it—had it on their pancakes or waffles on Sunday mornings. I continued my sugar maple sap gathering for a number of years after that; it's something you don't just forget.

The millrace was a place of other wonders for me too. About halfway back to the race head at the top of the bluff—which, by the way, was only about forty yards from the west side of the upper forty fields—I discovered a bee tree. It also was a maple tree and had a crack on the south side of the trunk, about fifteen feet off the ground, where the bees were coming and going from the tree. I could tell they had been there a long time because the wood and bark around the crack was smooth and shiny from all the bee traffic, with all those takeoffs and landings. Again, I just had to have some of that honey, so I developed this plan to get into the tree without cutting it down and destroying the bees. I figured I would wait until it got real cold so the bees would be dormant. I then built a small ladder from tree limbs to reach the crack. I really wasn't sure which way the honey was—up or down the tree—but after some deliberation, I figured it would be up from the crack. I bored four holes with the carpenter hand drill, forming a rectangle of about twelve by sixteen inches, and sure enough, the tree was only about an inch to an inch and a half thick at that place. I then screwed an eyebolt into the middle of it. Next, I took one of those small hand saws with about a four-inch cutting blade and a pistol-type grip and began to saw on about a forty-five-degree angle—wider on the outside of the cut than the inside—from hole to hole. It was a tough job, but I finally got it done. The true test of this plan was when I pulled on the eyebolt and the cut came loose so that I could reach some honey.

Wow! When I pulled the cut piece out, it was full of comb honey. The honey attached to the wood was shaped like large ribbon candy and dark in color. I was so excited I think I hollered! I had brought along a pail, although I never expected to get enough to fill it. After removing just the honey, I put the cut piece back in the tree and tied it tightly in place with a rope. I came back a number of times to ensure that it had not shifted. It wasn't long before I noticed that the bees had sealed the cut with wax from the inside, so I removed the rope. Each year after that, I would collect a new batch of honey; all I had to do was score the wax with a knife where the bees had resealed it, pull the cut section out by the eyebolt, and presto, there was the honey. Mom always canned the honey for us in pint jars so we could enjoy it all year long.

I went back to see that tree a few years ago, and it was gone; however, this past year, I found another bee tree, a really old maple, growing on the berm of the old millrace not thirty-five yards from where I'd discovered the first bee tree. I would bet my lunch money that this second hive is a swarm that is related to the original hive that I found years ago. Bees do that. If a hive gets too big, the worker bees feed some of the larvae what is called royal jelly, and they grow to become queens. Then, at the right time, one of them will fly high up in the air and become fertilized by drones. Once this is complete, the new queen will leave the hive, along with a large portion of the existing worker bees, and together, they seek out and establish a new hive. Now, this explanation may not be exactly how the system works, but it gives you an idea as to how bees build new colonies and expand their presence.

What has stayed with me all these years is how Mom and I worked together every year on these projects. I was so blessed to have a mother who supported and helped me with all the crazy schemes I used to come up with. Whatever I thought, whatever I wanted to learn, she was right there helping and teaching me.

# Chapter 22

# Special Places

There were certain places on Windale that were very special to me. They were places where I could go and leave the rest of the world behind, places where I could dream and fantasize about being whomever, doing whatever, or going wherever I wanted. They were solitary places, places where you very seldom saw other people, only the heart of nature. I loved those places, mostly because I could just be myself and not what others thought I should be. I only had myself to answer to; I was the only judge of myself and my actions. They were places where I took only my dog, Donnie, and my best friend, Bob Huck.

There were four of these special places. One was the millrace that I wrote about in the previous chapter; the other three were the cliff, the ravine, and the upper forty open acres, which I have written about somewhat before. Now that you have been introduced to these three new wonderful places, I would like to tell you about them and why they were so special.

The cliff, as I called it, was located east of the northern end of the millrace. Actually, it was the northern beginning of the bluff I described that ran the length of the millrace. Evitt's Creek flowed south directly into the north face of the bluff, and the bluff, being made up of mostly heavy shale, stopped the creek cold and turned it to the west, where the soil was softer and flatter. However, after hundreds or even thousands of years, the creek had eroded the bluff to the point where its face was almost vertical, thus my name the cliff. From the top of the bluff, then down its north face, to the creek was about two hundred feet consisting mainly of jagged shale and moss.

The most outstanding feature of the cliff was a hemlock grove that grew on its top and face. Eastern hemlocks grow well on north-facing slopes, and the cliff was just perfect for them. The grove on top of the cliff was about seventy-five yards deep and ran west to east for about two hundred yards to where it ended abruptly at a deep ravine running north to south. North-facing slopes also provide well for rhododendron and laurel, both of which also grew there. As you can imagine, the whole area was an evergreen forest with a few exceptions of some oaks and wild cherry. It was just magnificent. Those old hemlocks had been there for at least two hundred years, blocking out the sun, so the forest floor was void of any undergrowth except the rhododendron and laurel and moss—lots of moss, moss so thick that walking on it was like walking on pillows. Another plant that grew there was teaberry—yes, teaberry, just like the old type chewing gum. The plants were very small, an inch or so high, with only two or three leaves. The plant would flower in the spring and later give one small red teaberry that contained a few seeds and tasted just great when eaten.

All across the face of the cliff were small animal trails that switched back and forth down its face. One day, I decided to follow a trail that had fresh signs of deer tracks. After I was about halfway down to the creek, I became a little concerned about the pitch of the trail. However, I figured the worst that could happen would be having to go all the way down to the creek and then wading out to the other side. It didn't quite work out that way though. I was about halfway down when the trail kept getting smaller and smaller to the point where it was just going to disappear. At about 120 feet down, it was almost vertical, and a great fear of being on the edge of something with nothing to hold on to overcame me. I froze! I couldn't move, my hands were shaking, and I had this overwhelming feeling of panic. In my desperation, I clung to some exposed roots and held my ground. I could hear the water running below me, about seventy-five feet down, and I realized it was actually under me; I couldn't see the bottom of the cliff. I hadn't noticed that the creek had undermined the cliff at the bottom. I couldn't go down, and I couldn't go up. I was by myself and really frightened and confused, to say the least.

Finally, I began to gather my wits about me, and I remember telling myself that everything would be all right tomorrow; I just had to figure out how to get back up the cliff face without hooves. The narrow path I had come down was damp and, for the most part, covered with moss and dead hemlock needles. All the trails on the face of the cliff were usually wet due to a lack of direct sunlight. I told myself I had to start climbing up; I couldn't stay there, that was for sure. I literally dug my fingers into the ground to get a good grip and grabbed anything I could to pull myself up. Slowly, I started to move up the path; I probably looked like some kind of weird four-legged animal trying to slither like a snake. I tried to stay as low and close to the ground as I could. It took what seemed like an eternity, but I finally got to the top, with only a few minor hiccups—and some bloody fingers. I never tried any of those trails again, but the memory of that experience still haunts me a bit today. I also still have that fear of heights and of being on the edge of something. Every time it happens, I get that hollow feeling low in my stomach, pain in my groin, aches in my knees, and I freeze up for a moment like I did back then.

Something else that made the cliff special was cutting down a Christmas tree for our home there. For some years, I would climb an old hemlock, cut the top off, load it on a wagon, and take it home. Many times, it was snowing or had snowed, which made it just a beautiful time. Today, a number of hemlocks now have duel tops as a result of my taking the tops for Christmas trees those many years ago. I miss those simpler times and the quiet times when I used to sit on the cliff's edge, listening to the creek below and dreaming of my life to come. It's funny, though, because I used to hunt there, but I never remember killing anything. I'm sure I could have but chose otherwise.

The third special place was the upper forty pastures, which were discussed for the most part in chapter thirteen of this chronicle of my experiences. I'm sure they were also mentioned in other places and most likely will be later, so I will leave the upper forty at that.

The last place I want to present to you is the ravine. More specifically, this ravine began behind the barn, which was east of the main house. There were a number of other ravines that intersected it from the north and south and where the watershed flowed into it. I say this because it drained most of the eastern and southern parts of the farm. Located at the bottom of this ravine was a run that I don't recall ever having a name. The run always had water, so it was a place for many different flora and fauna. The ravine was very narrow at the bottom—mostly, twenty-five to thirty feet wide—and in a few places, there was only room for the run.

Just behind the barn about one hundred yards or so, there was the remnants of an old car; I have no idea how it got there or what the make was. It was located about ten yards up the south side of the ravine and was mostly covered by soil and debris, with trees growing up through it and all around it. Heavy, thick metal fenders could be seen, but not a whole lot more. The most interesting part about this old car was the huge old hog that lived in it. The hog had dug out all around it and lived inside the body of the car. It never did any harm that I knew of, and it didn't come near the house; it might have come to the barn, but I never saw it there. I just remember it being very big and keeping my distance from it when I did see it. It wasn't a wild boar but a domestic hog of some sort that had gone feral. It was there about three or four years, and then it was gone. I don't know what happened to it; most likely, someone hunting on the property shot it. If that was the case, I'll bet that meat was strong and tough after living on roots and acorns all those years.

Farther up the ravine, I found what was left of an old corduroy road; for those of you who are not familiar with this type of road, I offer the following explanation: corduroy roads were made of small hardwood logs two to four inches in diameter that were laid side by side on marshy ground; the logs enabled one to traverse such unstable ground with a cart or buggy without bogging down in the mud. I walked the ravine in 2009 and found a small portion of that road still intact. It had been covered over sometime in past years, then later uncovered due to erosion. Not too many logs were left and some of them were in somewhat of a disarray, but it's amazing that there were any logs left at all, given that they were laid down, I would estimate, over 150 years ago. They had all turned black but looked to be in fairly good condition. I always wondered why the road was there in the first place. It may have been used as a passage route from the main house through the ravine to where it ended at higher ground, which was more easily traveled. It also could have been that someone lived up in that area, which I later found out was most likely why it was built. I will explain all about that shortly.

Not too far up the Ravine from where I found the corduroy road, on its south side, was a monument tree—a huge old maple, which, for reasons unknown to me, was used as a survey or boundary marker. Driven into the tree about six feet from the ground were three very large spikes that protruded from the trunk about two to four inches. One of the spikes was located on the south side of the tree and the other two on the east and west sides. That old maple tree had been growing around them for many years, so there wasn't too much of them still showing. I should note that I also found another monument tree on the far northwest corner of Windale's property, which was a far distance from the one I'm talking about in the ravine. Again, it was a huge old tree, but this one was oak. In 2009, I found it again, so I looked at some old survey maps of the property. Sure enough, that monument tree marker is shown, but the one in the ravine is not, so I don't have any idea as to why it was there. When I found it again, also in 2009, that old tree was in pretty bad shape. Most of it had died, and it was only about twenty feet tall; I suspect it won't be alive for too many more years. This old monument tree probably isn't known by anyone else, so I took pictures and gave them to the owner of the property so she would have some record of it, and maybe someone will figure it out someday.

# Chapter 23

# The Old Cabin Site

Now I would like to tell you about the most fascinating find I ever made on the farm. As a boy, I envisioned myself as an explorer, looking for things no one knew anything about. To me, I was the first to tread this land that I lived on. I guess I was to a degree, because it had been a very long time since anyone had walked those lands. I suspect an occasional hunter had been through the ravine, but it really wasn't a good place to hunt—there wasn't much visibility. Besides, I'm sure they weren't looking for unusual things or places; they would have been looking for game. It was the unusual that I was looking for. I have always had the ability to spot something different, whether it be by shape, color, something out of place, or different from the norm.

I gathered reference and guide books to identify an unusual rock or fossil or what type of bird I had seen or tree I had found. All that information stuck like glue in my head, especially the birds and trees. I could identify trees by their structure, leaf shape, or bark type, any season of the year. I knew birds by their color or shape or the way they flew; I knew their songs and calls and what habitat they liked. I just lived for that stuff. This was one thing that I excelled in and was better at than most people.

One day when looking for fossils on shale banks in the ravine just above where the monument tree was located, I found a very large free-flowing spring that appeared to be the headwaters of the run. I should also mention that the ravine, since its start at the barn, gradually swung from an easterly direction to a more northerly direction before ending. This spring was about thirty yards east of the ravine, just before the ravine ended. I found it mainly because I was following the run and not the ravine. A spring like this one really brings in the animals, and there were tracks everywhere. I found deer, foxes, and coon, just to mention a few. I'm sure there were frogs and crayfish also, because the run had them from beginning to end; the run also had small minnows in most of its pools as well as salamanders. It was hard to turn a rock and not find something under it.

The spring was located in a swale just below a small bluff above the ravine. It was about a quarter of a mile below a quick-rising ridge to the east of which was the property line for the farm. This property line was the one that had the second monument tree. That ridge was very rocky and difficult to climb; its face was strewn with many dead American chestnut trees that had died off from the blight in the last thirty years or so. Occasionally, you would find a young chestnut sprout that had come up from the old roots. But they didn't live very long, just long enough to grow about ten or twelve feet tall.

Having found the spring and knowing what I could see there, I went back many times just to spot the animals. One time in the early spring, I was walking around the bluff and found some narcissi growing, which I thought was unusual out there in the woods in the middle of nowhere. This got me more curious, and then I found an old apple tree that was just starting to bloom. Then I spotted it—an unusual formation of stones. Upon further investigation, I realized it was possibly an old foundation to a long-forgotten cabin. There wasn't anything else there but the stones, so I figured it must have been very old. I was so excited, and my imagination was running wild. It all fit—the spring, the apple tree, the narcissi, and now the rock foundation. Someone had lived there a long time ago, most likely because of the spring, which would have provided a constant supply of water and game all year long. The cabin site also gave reason for the old corduroy road. This may seem strange, but for the rest of the time I lived at Windale, I didn't tell anyone about what I had found. That find was my place. I was the only one who knew about it, and I wasn't going to share it with anyone—just keep it to myself. I'm not sure why, but that's what I did. Some years later, I did break that promise to myself, though, but just once, and that was when I showed Bob, my best friend, where it was.

Jumping forward to 1997, I went back to Cumberland to celebrate my fiftieth Fort Hill High School class reunion, and while I was there, I decided to take some time to visit the old home place. My intent for the visit was to show Linda, my wife, some of these beautiful places I have been writing about. I took her down to the old millrace; I took her up to the cliff. I took her to the upper forty acres, and then my plan was to show her the old cabin site, which I had never shown to anyone before but my friend Bob. I wanted to share with her the beautiful memories I had of those places. Well, you guessed it, I couldn't find it. I looked all over that ravine to no avail. I was astonished when I couldn't find it; after all, it had only been sixty-some years! Not finding that cabin site really challenged me. Had I just imagined the whole thing? Was it just a figment of my imagination? My saving grace was when Bob assured me that I had indeed found it, because he said I had showed it to him. But he remembered it on the left side of the ravine, not on the right side where I had been looking for it. Time was short, so I had to leave Cumberland without another chance to search for the site.

I now had a mission to find that site, which I still believed was on the right side of the ravine. Two summers later, Linda and I made arrangements with Mary Miltenberger, who owns the old house and farm that is now a bed-and-breakfast named "Terra Angelica", to come visit for a month. I wanted to reacquaint myself with the wonderful life I had lived while growing up there, find that cabin site, and start this book. I had mental images of where the cabin site was; I knew it sat on a bluff, which I could see to my right. I could envision the spring flowing down from the right just below the bluff and an old apple tree standing to the west of the site. I knew if I looked for those characteristics to my right as I progressed up the ravine, I would find it.

I first talked to Charlie O'Neal, an old childhood friend who was building a home near the farm, and then Vandy, a neighbor just up the road whom I had just met, both of whom had hunted on the farm over the years. I asked them if they had ever come across the old cabin site. Vandy thought maybe he had seen it and suggested we go searching for it. He had an old four-wheel-drive farm truck, so we all piled in and drove up an old log road from the northeast corner of the upper forty until we couldn't go any farther and then started walking to where Vandy thought it might be. We weren't coming up the ravine, so everything looked different to me. After a lot of stumbling around, I noticed some large rocks that looked to be the foundation rocks, and sure enough, after some digging, we confirmed that they were part of the old foundation. The old apple tree was gone, so I began looking for the spring, and it was right where I thought it would be. I was just elated and couldn't wait to tell Linda and Mary of the discovery.

The next day, I took Linda to the site, and we dug around a little with hand shovels just to see if we could find anything interesting. We found a lot of handmade nails and a few pottery shards, some bone buttons, a kitchen knife, and a pair of scissors. We found enough to confirm that, at one time, someone had lived in what was probably a wooden cabin. We also found some bricks that were of the same nature as those of the main farmhouse, which were probably from the cabin's chimney.

We returned to Mary's house, and she too was excited and suggested we rent a metal detector to scan the area. The next day, we did just that and found a lot more nails and other unknown metal pieces. I also scanned the whole area, and there was evidence of many other metal objects buried there. Upon returning to the farmhouse and discussing the day's events, I suggested to Mary that this cabin site and the other beautiful special places that I loved should be restored and become part of the B and B. With the development of a few trails, other people could hike the farm and enjoy the beauty and history it offered. Mary agreed, so Linda and I made plans right then to return the following year for two months and begin the project. During the summer of 2010, we did in fact restore the millrace with a toe path on its berm, which leads to a walking trail up the bluff's spine to the top of the cliff and then continues to the upper forty pastures and its beautiful view of Evitt's Valley looking toward Cumberland.

Our plan for 2011 was to do a formal dig at the cabin site, restore its foundation, and then, if time permitted, complete a walking trail to that site as well. Considering the future of the site, I believed I had located the privy location that serviced the cabin, and if that were the case, we would spend another summer excavating that. The privy would prove to be an excellent place to find artifacts, because back then, people used them to dispose of broken or unwanted possessions. I also hoped to put in a second walking trail to the old cabin site, which would start at the main house and travel up the ravine to the spring location and then on to the cabin site.

Linda and I did return in 2011 to perform the formal dig of the site as we had planed the previous summer. The project took six weeks to complete. We found many artifacts that have led us to believe the cabin was probably built sometime in the late 1700s or early 1800s. In the process of the excavation, we discovered almost all the original foundation stones, which enabled us to rebuild the foundation to a dimension of about sixteen by twenty feet. We found many china and pottery chards; knives, forks, and spoons with bone or wood handles; coins; and many other pieces. After restoring the foundation and the dig site, Linda and I restored the spring to its original design of the first people who lived there. We are now in the process of identifying and cataloging all the excavated items. As of July 2012, all the artifacts have been restored, and efforts are underway to exhibit them in the Cumberland area.

# Chapter 24

# Family

We all understand the relationships that make up a family. I had a fairly large family while growing up. There was Mom and Dad; my two sisters, Christina and Gloria Kay; and my brother, David. Then there was my grandmother and grandfather Windish and, most of the time, my grandmother and grandfather Stacey, for a total of ten in the house. If you have never been a part of a large family, you may not realize that it takes a lot of sharing and understanding to make it all work. Like the old TV show *The Walton's*, in my family, each individual played a unique part overall; however, there were subgroups in the family that also played an important role in the harmony necessary to getting along with one another.

For example, my grandmother and grandfather Windish and I were one group. My grandmother Windish and my sister Gloria were another. Then there was my sister Christina and my grandmom Stacey or my mother with all of us children and so on. I must say too that there were other relationships that were not always in the best interest of the family, like the one my father and I had for some years, but that's another story.

When I think about our family from a different perspective, there were actually three families living in the same house, each of equal importance, each having their own lives, and each having their own way of living, yet they were one in the same, one family, like the three sides of a triangle forms one musical instrument, separate yet bound together as one. The great thing about it was, for the most part, the arrangement worked and we were happy.

All the women of our family were strong and determined people, but each in her own special way. Mom was a problem solver and catalyst who held everything together; Grandmother Windish was a strong woman of God, keeping the Christian discipline; and Grandmother Stacey was an independent interior decorator in downtown Philadelphia and a successful businesswoman, to the extent that, during World War I, the U.S. government asked her to shut down her interior decorating business and make canvas airplane wings for them. I would say that all three of them were the corners of the family triangle I talked about; they were connected to each other like the three sides of a triangle, forming one family unit. They were connected in such a way that held everything together and made everything work. However, this is not to say that differences did not arise between them, but those differences were always settled and never interfered with the harmony of the family or the security of us children.

In essence, I had three mothers. My mom, whom I'm sure liked me best, was always there for me and always understood me. My second mom, Grandmother Windish, acted as my spiritual teacher and moral compass, and my third mom, Grandmother Stacey, taught me discipline and honor. I respected and loved each one of them. The three of them were a refuge of love and respect for me that drew me into a place where I found contentment and peace. They all had one common objective—to nurture the family—and they each approached that objective in a different way. Growing up with those three women during my formative years probably had more to do with who I became as a young man than anything else I can think of.

My mother, though, was the person who taught me the practical things of life; she made sure that no matter what situation I got myself into in life, I could find a practical solution. She taught me how to do laundry, cook, iron, and clean, as well as all the other things I mentioned above. As an example, when I was in the army and attending school at Fort Devens in Massachusetts, I, of course, was always out of money. I had my car with me, an MGA, but no money for gas. I decided to hang out a shingle in the barracks advertising that I would iron uniforms for two bucks each. My buddy Phil Finely and I never had to worry about gas money—or beer money, for that matter—after that. Mom was a practical person; I learned how to save money, not want things I didn't need, and always be generous—to be a giver. She taught me how to take care of myself, be aware of my needs, deal with the unexpected, and be kind. She was always there for me when I needed her, and I loved her deeply.

No one in the world knew me any better than Mom. I now know she understood me, how I looked at the world, and the things that were important to me. She understood my love for nature and the difficulty I had being part of the norm. She knew I had a hunger to see more of the world. When I was in ninth grade, fourteen years old, the only place I had ever been other than the farm was Beach Haven, New Jersey, and I wouldn't want anyone to think that wasn't a big deal, because it was, but I wanted to see more. Grandmother Stacey used to go to Miami, Florida, every winter after Grandfather Stacey died in 1949. She always took the train down and back, but one year, Mom decided to drive down to Miami to pick her up and bring her home. Mom also decided to take me with her on the trip, so she went to Fort Hill High School to get authorization for me to be out of school. The school granted her permission, stating that I would probably learn more on the trip than I would by attending classes. I'm not sure what that meant—remember, I wasn't too good of a student—but maybe they thought I would experience more. I was just thrilled beyond explanation and could think of nothing else for weeks.

About two weeks before we were scheduled to leave, I had an accident; I was running and fell on the corner of a brick and punched a hole in my left kneecap. I just knew it was all over, that I would never be able to go to Florida. Thankfully it healed up quickly and I got to go, because that trip was the most wonderful thing that had ever happened to me. I saw things I had only read about in books or had seen on my View-Master, and the answers to so many questions just flooded in. I probably drove my mom nuts talking about all the things and places I was seeing—tobacco fields, cotton fields, orange groves, palm trees, coconuts, strange birds I had never seen. It was just astounding.

After arriving in Miami, we stayed with my grandmother for a few days in her apartment. We went out to eat at an Automat, which I never did at home, and I had Salisbury steak. I loved it so much I had it every night! Yes, me, a person who didn't like to eat meat. I bought a coconut that was carved into a monkey's face, which, by the way, I still have today. I also picked up coconuts that had fallen off the trees around Grandmom's apartment and brought them all home.

The one thing that trip set in my mind was how much I loved the South, especially Florida. I now live in the South—on Edisto Island in South Carolina—and have traveled to Florida every year since 1979. I actually wrote a great deal of this book while living on Marathon Key during the winter. As you can see, my mother understood me well and did all she could to fulfill the needs I had that would eventually guide my life in the direction she knew I wanted it to go. Her nurturing and understanding sculpted my young mind to follow my dreams and be the best I could be. Mom passed away in 1995 at the age of ninety two and I still miss her so.

# Chapter 25

# My Grandmother Windish

Grandmother Windish was a great mentor for me. When it came to faith in God, she was a rock, a deeply religious woman who had a tremendous faith, and she was full of the wisdom of God. She was my refuge from confusion and the bad things that happened to me, a place of peace, someone I could run to when I didn't want to go to my parents. I loved her deeply. She spent a lot of time teaching me to have faith and to understand the wisdom in the Bible. I didn't realize it until years later, but she had a profound impact on my life. During my innocence, she was my moral compass, teaching me and moving me in a direction of understanding that allowed me to develop the faith I have today. She was a holy person, a believer, a disciple.

Every Sunday, she would take me to Sunday school and church at Centenary Methodist. I remember sitting with her in church and looking up at her when she sang. She was a medium-sized woman, with a beautiful face and red hair, who always dressed well for church, but she had one flaw. She had a terrible singing voice. It was high and squeaky and off-key. That never stopped her from singing, however. It was her intent to make a joyful noise to the Lord, and she did. She told me to always sing with all my heart when praising the Lord. She said, "He doesn't care how it sounds; he only cares that you do it, so sing!"

My parents didn't go to church—actually, no one else in the family did except my grandmother Windish and us children. Every Sunday, Grandmom, as I called her, would get herself ready to go to church and expected my mother to get us kids ready. My father would drive us up to Centenary and leave us off for Sunday school and the church service, then pick us up at noon when it was over. Dad was a heavy smoker—and I mean *heavy*. It wasn't often that he was seen without a cigarette. He would arrive at the church early and sit in the car with the windows closed and smoke; I guess he thought he could get more out of his smoking if he didn't let the smoke escape. That was great for him and terrible for us kids. A lot of my sickness as a child, as I have said before, I'm sure was the result of secondhand smoke.

Centenary was and still is a country church, a traditional church where God, Jesus Christ, and the Holy Spirit are the center of everything in a very conservative way. Centenary, at that time, was one of three churches on a circuit that shared a pastor; the other two were Zion Church on Hazen Road and another very small church on Mason Road, which I can't remember the name now. It was on top of the hill just after the big swimming hole and just before the Fagan farm. If I remember right, one of the three churches didn't have a service each week, which made the rounds through all three churches. On the Sundays the Centenary didn't have a service, my sister Christina and I would walk to the little church on the hill and attend there. Centenary Methodist is the only church still remaining out of the three.

There was always a lot of music, mostly old-time gospel music. The hymns we sung were the kind that if you went to church in the forties and fifties you learned by heart and still could sing them today without looking at the hymnal. I have nothing but the fondest memories of Centenary Methodist Church.

In the summer of 2010, while I was back at Windale working on restoring the millrace, a wonderful thing happened to me. Centenary's pastor was reassigned, and there was a problem in finding a replacement. I am a certified lay speaker for the Methodist Church in South Carolina, so I volunteered to fill in, and they accepted. I can't tell you what a thrill it was to go back to that bedrock church of my life and preach. I preached three Sundays, one of which was the Sunday of their church picnic out near Rocky Gap State Park. I was able to preach under a pavilion with nothing but Mother Nature all around. It was a time I will never forget. Another great experience I had when I went back to Centenary was seeing many of the kids I grew up with who are now married and attend the church with their children and grandchildren.

For the most part, the members of Centenary were country people. The church practically sat on the Mason Dixon Line, so the congregation hailed from both Pennsylvania and Maryland. It was a great place for the community to come together, not only for church and Sunday school, but also for dinners and celebrations. It was great for us kids too. Since we didn't all live in the same state, we went to different schools, and coming together at church gave us the chance to plan activities inside and outside of the church—for example, playing basketball in the church league. In the summer and fall, we would make plans to play touch football or softball up at Lake Gordon on the green that was located there. Another thing we did at least once every summer was to climb Evitt's Mountain; most of the time, there were between fifteen and twenty of us kids who made the climb. It took all afternoon to get to the top. The gas company had laid a line over the mountain, and that's the trail we followed to get up. It was a difficult climb, but most made it to the top. Once on the top, there was a dirt service road running north and south, and if we followed it about a half mile, we would come to a high-beacon light tower, maybe 150 feet tall, that was there to warn aircraft of the mountain's presence.

The tower was located under a major flight path for both commercial and military aircraft. It is interesting to note that, during those years while the Cold War was going on, the government had aircraft-spotting stations located under that flight path. One was located on Bedford Road, Route 220, and was manned by volunteers from the community every day. When I was inside it one time, I saw the walls were covered with pictures and designs of all kinds of aircraft, both American and Russian, to enable the spotters to identify enemy aircraft. It seems somewhat antiquated now, but that's how it was done.

Anyway, once atop Evitt's, we had a spectacular view of Evitt's Valley North and South as well as across the valley to Will's Mountain. After a good rest, we would start our descent back down the pipeline, and when we reached Bottle Run, we knew where we had left our bikes was close.

Getting back to Grandmother Windish, she was responsible for the foundation on which my faith was built. As I mentioned in the prologue, I believe there are certain passages we go through in our lives that form the person whom we become. My time with my grandmother was one of those passages. During that formative time with her, she laid out certain rules for me to follow. I was to pray every night, so she taught me to recite the Lord's Prayer, be thankful for all I had, and ask God to bless all those I loved. I was never to take the Lord's name in vain, and if I slipped, she would come down hard on me. She said I should never hate anyone regardless of who they were and that I should love others. She taught me to love myself as a child of God, and if I did, He would always take care of me. I still believe that today, and God does take care of me. Grandmom would teach me all she knew about Jesus one way or another.

My grandmother and grandfather's bedroom was located just upstairs on the northwest corner of the house. In the winter, it was probably the coldest of all the bedrooms. They had a double-sized featherbed. For those who don't know about featherbeds, when you make the bed, you fluff the feather mattress up and cover it with a feather comforter so the bed looks like a huge marshmallow. I just loved getting in it with them and snuggling under all the covers to keep warm.

When I was still a young boy, I spent a lot of time in my room listening to programs on the radio. My room was catty-corner across the hall from theirs, so when I heard them coming up the stairs to go to bed, which was usually pretty early in the evening, I would put on my pajamas and go over to their room and get in bed between the two of them. Oh my, what a wonderful feeling of security and comfort that was. Pop was a big man, and he always lay on the right side of the bed facing the doorway, so I only could see his big back. Grandmom lay on the left side, and there I was, snugly ensconced between them. All the lights would be turned out except for one of those picture lights made of green glass with an inlaid picture of a beautiful iris plant in bloom, and the radio would be dialed to a Christian station in Long Beach,

California, that would only come through at night. Grandmom and I would lay there listening to the preacher preaching and the choir singing for about an hour, and then I would go back to my own room. Pop was usually long gone by the time I left. Though so long ago, those nights are still so clear, so memorable. I can still feel their warmth, hear Pop's deep breathing and Grandmom singing along with the choir. She always kissed me and told me I was a good boy and that she was proud of me.

One other story I want to tell you about Grandmom pertains to attending camp meeting services. Every summer, usually in July, local churches would hold camp meeting services about half a mile down the road at the Union Grove Camp Grounds. My grandmother loved camp meeting time; no matter what church was having services, she would go. She always walked down to the campground to the service, which usually started around seven thirty in the evening—still daylight. Most times, she took me with her, which wasn't a problem for me. I just loved being there with all those good people, listening to those fiery preachers, especially under that big Quonset hut–shaped building surrounded by huge old oak trees. It was just wonderful! I remember a big choir loft, large altar, and tall wooden pulpit, which probably appeared larger to me because I was so small at the time. Sawdust covered the floor, and the sides of the building were all open, with roll-down canvas curtains on three sides in case the weather turned bad.

I remember hearing the old-time gospel songs and watching as people gave themselves to Jesus up at the altar—all to the wonderful nightly sounds of summer. I always wanted to walk up that aisle to that altar and tell Jesus I loved him, but I just couldn't bring myself do it at the time. I knew in my heart, though, that Jesus knew I wanted to do it. Those times taught me about God and about His creations and that I really didn't have anything to fear from God or the people who loved him.

The service was usually over by about nine, so Grandmom and I would start our trek home. She would talk about the service and what was said, and I just listened. We walked along in the dark, again listening to all those wonderful nighttime sounds, while holding hands. My grandmom's hands were always warm and so soft. Soon we were home, and life with her once again had left its mark. She was and always will be a saint to me and the foundation of my faith. How fortunate I was to have her in my life to enable me with her faith and wisdom.

There was another side to Grandmom that I haven't mentioned— a fiery side, a fun side. After all, she did have red hair! She smoked cigarettes, drove a car, had some pretty pointed opinions about how things should be, and loved a good joke. She also loved to play cards and taught me all the games she knew, but we never—and I mean *never*—played for money or on a Sunday. I remember a couple of stories that were often told about her, one of which was when we moved to Windale and she drove carloads of stuff out to the new house. On one trip, Grandmom decided to bring the family cat along. Well, it didn't turn out so well. The cat, not being used to being in a car, became very nervous and began wandering around the top of the front seat. The cat decided to move his bowels in protest of the trip right down her back, and Grandmom had to drive about ten miles in that condition! Grandmom got pretty upset when that story was told again and people would laugh at her.

Another story relating to Grandmom was one day when she went up on the hill just above the house for a short walk and all of a sudden came running back to the house screaming about a cat. After they settled her down, she told them she had seen a lion. She explained that she was walking up the tractor path to look at the blooming dogwoods and redbuds, and when she saw this large cat jump down out of a redbud tree, she turned tail and ran back to the house. I'm not sure anyone really trusted her story, because mountain lions hadn't been seen in that area for many a year. However, if she said she saw a mountain lion, I believed her, and she never went up on the hill again, which tells you something. As a side note, there have been a number of big cats spotted in the last couple of years, one of which was seen by my friend Merwin Hast, the son of Game Warden Hast, whom I mentioned earlier.

In testimony, I would like to say that we are given many gifts during the course of our lifetimes, and they are special only to us. They are unique to only us personally and should be used wisely, not wasted on the quest for additional wealth or possessions. We should see these gifts for their value, not just for us, but also for others who have not had the opportunity to be a part of them. Looking back on all this, I know in my heart that the gifts that came to me from living at Windale were a result of the supportive family I had, the love I have for nature, and the wonder I feel for all of God's creations. The passion I have for God's creations led me to wander that farm and fired my imagination so I could see its beauty as it was meant to be seen, discover what was there to be discovered, and dream and plan for things to come as they unfolded later in my life. Our past can become part of our future if it is used to grow and give perspective to who we've become and how it affects others who enter into our lives. I have learned that life—in spite of the trials we bare, the crosses we carry, the fears we suffer, the tragedies we endure, and the failures we undergo—is an absolutely beautiful and fulfilling adventure, not to be destroyed by insecurity, greed, or the opinions of others. Life should be lived in its entirety every waking day of our lives. I thank God for the gifts he has presented to me throughout my lifetime and for the opportunity to share them with all who care.

The following poem " FIREFLY" expresses how I found that the smallest gifts of nature may serve as an allegory to enlighten and motivate us to better understand life's journey.

\* \* \*

## *Firefly*

—George Windish, February 2009

*Thinking back, looking deep into the corners of my heart*
*Passing through the vale of life's many celestial trips*
*Reaching and feeling to once again find youth's passion*
*I find that life's old memories will give up their treasured secrets*

*Secrets that once again rouse and fire the depth of our emotions*
*Carry us back to times long abandoned, places once cherished*
*They quicken our blood, sharpen our senses, and expand our thoughts*
*Remind us of who we are, where we have traveled, whom we have loved*

*Secrets, seen only with clarity, belonging to us, treasures held*
*Emerging from our souls as fresh, cool water from a forgotten spring*
*They cleanse our bodies of the scales from life's failures and trials*
*Bringing meaning to all time past, showing why hope eternally flows*

*Life only allows the past that has shaped and sculpted us to*
 *remain*
*All else is hidden as behind the wisp of lost time, uncertainty,*
 *and fear*
*We should embrace life's gifts given, keeping them polished, at*
 *the ready*

Holding them up proudly, sharing them unselfishly with those
   to come

As the firefly in the stillness and quiet of a warm early evening
   in June
Without sound, slowly rises from the cool earth and begins to
   glow softly
Then flash with rhythm, giving direction, a gift carried from
   its past
So we too should use this creature's way to carry forth our legacy
   and our flame

# Chapter 26

# Long Beach Island

Up to the time that I was fifteen years old, the summer was spent visiting my grandmother and grandfather Stacey in Long Beach Island, New Jersey. My grandparents had a home on Jerome Avenue in Beach Haven Park that they built in 1929. My sister Christina and I were very close siblings and constant companions, especially when I was younger. We told each other everything and trusted each other completely, which created a loving bond between us that is still strong today. We did chores together, ate together, spent our days on the beach together, swam together, rode bikes together, and went to the post office as well as church together. We also went clamming and crabbing for both hard- and soft-shell crabs and fished in the surf for bluefish. I would be remiss if I didn't mention that Chris was a great body surfer and taught me how to be one too. We did all those things that children do together at the Jersey Shore in the summer. But there is one more thing in particular we used to do that I would like to tell you about—meeting the fishing boats that came in every day early in the morning.

*Christina and I at Beach Haven*

At that time, there were Swedish fishermen living on Long Beach Island who had their fishnets set up a few miles off the coast. Each day, they would go out to the nets at first light and gather their catch. The boat they used was about thirty feet long and shaped like an ark—wide in the middle and high at the bow and stern. Actually, it looked like either end of the boat could be the bow or stern and may have been designed so the tiller could be attached to both ends, with the top completely open. Eight fishermen manned the boat, and as I remember, it was attached to a mooring post located just beyond the breaker. The boat was beached on the sand when not in use with a line to the mooring post. To launch the boat, the crew would push the boat across the sand on cedar logs that rolled to the water's edge, then pull it to the mooring post through the breakers using an attached rope. Once past the breakers, they would row the boat to the netting grounds. Upon returning, they would row the boat through the breakers and then beach it on the cedar logs so it was ready for the next morning. It was an amazing process done by amazing, strong men.

Now back to why we would go up to meet the boats in the first place. Grandmother Stacey was a frugal person, so a lot of the food we ate came from the sea and the bay. That which came from the sea mostly came from those boats. Once the fisherman had secured the boat, they would separate the fish into large baskets. While sorting the fish, they would throw any kinds or sizes of fish they didn't want over the side of the boat, and it was our job to retrieve the fish that Grandmom wanted ahead of all the other people who were also there for free fish. As I recall, we were pretty good at it; we were small and fast and could grab the type of fish Grandmom wanted. We quickly stuffed the fish we gathered into a burlap sack we had brought with us and then headed home.

There were two fish markets on the island, each having its own boat, as I described earlier, that caught and sold fish. Chris and I went to the closest one, which was about eight or ten blocks south of where we lived on Jerome Avenue. That way of life is completely gone now—the nets, the boats, the markets, and most likely, the fishermen. That whole culture is gone forever mainly due to the loss of the Swedish population living on Long Beach Island, the industry becoming motorized, and the depletion of our fisheries.

Some of the years we spent together at Beach Haven were the summers of the great polio epidemics. For some unknown reason, it seems no one ever got polio at the beach, and I thank God for that. I remember hearing about the epidemics in Philadelphia, which was only fifty or sixty miles away, but never hearing of anyone at the beach coming down with it. Maybe that's why Mom and Dad used to send us down there—as a precaution. Then again, it may have been that, with four kids, it was good to get at least two of us out of the house for a while. Those were formative years for me, and being nurtured by my grandparents helped me to understand their generation and the culture they grew up in, their families and the lives they lived, and especially why my mother was the wonderful person she was.

To get a complete understanding of how wonderful it was to spend our summers at the beach in Beach Haven, New Jersey, I suggest you read *Jetty Walker*, the book my sister (Christina Snyder) wrote about our time there. It's a great read!

# Chapter 27

# Seasons

One great thing about living in Western Maryland is the distinctive difference between the seasons; each season has its own special characteristics. Unlike other places I've lived where winter is long with a short spring or summer, it has more of a long spring than summer.

I have always felt gifted to be able to recognize the uniqueness of each season, that detail which makes it special from others. The following poem "SEASONS" is a reflection of that detail they each exhibit.

\* \* \*

## Seasons

*—George Windish, 1998*

*Given the time to consider the season*
*What is it that comes to mind?*

*We search our heart for wisdom and reason*
*Which somehow we're unable to find*

*Why do we miss its joy and spirit*
*Even though better we know*
*Could it be we just don't hear it?*
*Or maybe our sight is too slow*

### Spring
*Given the time to consider the season*
*What is it that comes to mind?*
*We search our heart for wisdom and reason*
*Which somehow we're unable to find*

*The smell of the rain as it warms the soil*
*Awakening the sleeping earth*
*On early warm days we physically toil*
*Thinking of newness and birth*

*Bright-colored blossoms begin to appear*
*Innocent and tender to frost*
*Promising renewal and hope each year*
*Tricked by warmth are quickly lost*

*Our thoughts of ageless youth return*
*Remembering sweetness and love*
*Seeing our life now brings concerns*
*Believing, hoping, and rising above*

# Seasons

While planting, sowing, and caring, we sing
As billowing mounts of clouds float by
We hurry by the nymph of spring
Till too late we see the summer sky


## Summer

Given the time to consider the season
What is it that comes to mind?
We search our heart for wisdom and reason
Which somehow we're unable to find

Seductive summer by the hand do we take
Meeting her every caress
She provides and gives for our sake
Clothed in her floral dress

Long days urge the sun's early light
Causing the land to smell sweet
Signaling and guiding northern flight
On strong wings to a rhythmic beat

Cicadas calling to announce their arrival
With leaves now green and full
Quickly lay eggs to ensure their survival
Before the days are much too cool

Cool lakes are now quiet and warm
Nights filled with the whip-poor-will's call
Magic lightning bugs rising in swarm
Carry our thoughts toward fall

*Fall*

Given the time to consider the season
What is it that comes to mind?
We search our hearts for wisdom and reason
Which somehow we're unable to find

Huge and gold comes the harvest moon
Man's features showing so clear
Easily blending with the night's tune
The allusion of being so near

Suddenly all the martins are gone
The rich, wavy fields turn gold
Less singing birds we hear at dawn
Sweet summer's sure end is told

Leaves now dressed in orange and yellow
Pumpkin and gourd they lie
Days have become clear and mellow
Bringing thoughts of turkey and pie

Days grow short and trees are bare
Long shadows early they cast
Nights are longer with frost in the air
Making us long for the past

*Winter*

Given the time to consider the season
What is it that comes to mind?
We search our heart for wisdom and reason
Which somehow we're unable to find

# Seasons

*The soft falling snow and its blanket of white*
*Quiet deer standing among trees*
*A bright-red cardinal quickened by flight*
*Field mice snuggled in brown fall leaves*

*Wind quietly singing through long needle pines*
*Crawling crowfoot prone on the forest floor*
*Craggy oaks stripped of leafy signs*
*Prickly green holly, red berries galore*

*Smoke from the chimney so slowly it curls*
*Family dinner about to begin*
*Lights in the windows shining like pearls*
*Warming those hearts within*

*Sun quickly slipping just out of sight*
*Bowing to nature's desire*
*Mother Earth, by turning oh so slight*
*Displays momentarily her winter fire*

*Darkness moves slowly to cover our sight*
*Soothing both mammal and fowl*
*Raising the moon to her crescent height*
*Reveals the flight of an owl*

*Stars rotating within a beautiful spiral*
*Mythical forms may be*
*Shimmering and blinking bright like coral*
*Part of the heavenly sea*

*Given the time to consider the season*
*What is it that comes to mind?*
*If we open our heart to wisdom and reason*
*So easy the answers we find*

Spring at Windale was so full of new life, with the birds returning and all the other great natural things occurring, I was quickly overwhelmed and could think of nothing else. Some would call it spring fever; I would call it love, a love for all creation being renewed. I really think the best way for me to tell you how I felt about spring is to let you read a poem I wrote back in March 2000 while on a return flight from Germany, where I had been on business. I dedicate this writing to my wife, Linda, who has taught me that love will calm my anger and show me the way to put my soul into words.

\* \* \*

## *Awaiting Spring*

—*George Windish, March 2000*

*As I long for change, the northwest wind still comes cold*
*Deep, drifted snow lies in shadows and mountain valleys*
*Soon, though, the tilt of Mother Earth will change winter's grip*
*The excitement I feel is reverent and full of wonder*

*Ice on the pond has become brittle and soft, lacking strength*
*It can no longer hold the creatures below captive with its shield*
*Peepers sing as though they were fools, stealing time from winter,*
*minute by minute*
*Hailing spring, they lay their precious eggs with the wisdom of*
*generations*

Hollow stumps, water filled from melted snow, provide for
Gestating white-tailed deer as they drink timidly of winter's gift
All of the woodland animals now move with a certainty of purpose
Only those of hibernation are still slow to embrace change

The creek water, now alive with rage, is heavy within its banks
Tree roots grab at its wash, but to no avail
Nothing can hold her now; destiny must be met, the cycle fulfilled
Fields must flood, the earth watered, leaving silt for summer's bounty

An old familiar but forgotten fragrance now travels on the air
Dampness forming on cold stones whispers lightly of a new beginning
Unsure winds begin to compete for what is to come
Inpatients brings dreams of coming warm days of escape

Fulfilling our need, Sol brings forth the first temperate days of glory
All rush to the openness, as if from caves of winter gloom
The freedom felt is elation and joy, which ransoms our senses
Nature's symphony so intently presented now through sight and sound

Within the darkness, silver frost tries to stop spring's rush, but is
        destined to fail
Quickly, it is soothed by sun and time, becoming morning dew
All forms of buds transform into life, presenting flowers and leaves
Tubers and bulbs push forth their miracle with ease and certainty

School is my prison now, wanting only freedom of all bonds
Every moment of gifted time is carefully planned, completely
        cherished
Each day will bring a new adventure, exploration, and knowledge

*I can no longer obey; I am in rebellion with those who wish to hold me*

*Wanting so to feel and see all changes momentarily rushing toward me*
*My heart bursts with thoughts, emotions, excitement, and love*
*Sleep is elusive, wasteful, consuming, with all there is to do, to feel, to loose*
*I must not waste precious understanding; it must be clear, for never again will this moment be*

*By now I am lost in the love of God's creations*
*I travel the woodlands and meadows searching for my place in it all*
*Now knowing the secrets of plants both great and small*
*I become one with them convinced now of their place in my life*

*Eagerly, I anticipate swallows, their arrival being proof of the promise*
*Their ease of flight and sleek beauty a wonder to me*
*How precious their nests with young, how skillfully constructed*
*I love them so; they have become part of my inspiration, my hope*

*Soon, following the swallows, come orioles, with their suits of color*
*Skillfully, they build perfect baskets of horsehair, lichen, and grass*
*Securely attached by beak and foot to graceful ends of giant spreading elm branches*
*Hanging free in the wind, swaying gently without harm to egg or fledgling*

*More than a century dug, the millrace parallels the clear creek's flow*
*Now, full with growth, it is home to bluebells, skunk cabbage,*
    *and ferns*
*Silver maples, blooming, drop crimson flower petals softly like snow*
*Wet weather springs seep from its banks to form rivulets of silver*

*Treading old log roads, I follow them with excitement, with wonder*
*Leading to the ghosts of pioneers past, where ancient gnarled*
    *apple trees grow*
*Lost in time, they bloom with pink-and-white splendor, which*
    *fall like tears*
*Surly there will be springs of cool, sweet water near*

*Traveling old paths where once great chestnuts grew*
*Hopeful saplings struggling for life from old roots, only a re-*
    *minder of past magnificence*
*Sharp ravines run like wrinkles in the land, presenting their mystery*
*Historic fossils appear at the foot of shale banks, exposed by*
    *winter freeze*

*The land is now warm and flooded with new life*
*Nature's promise has been fulfilled with humility and grace*
*Earth has once more given birth to a new generation*
*All is well in my heart as I hear the music of her life*

*I have moved closer now to those who went before me*
*Understanding their awe of feeling the oneness with all living things*
*I know now I am not alone but a part of a great spirit*
*My place in all time is secure through the wisdom of loving*
    *all creations*

*I will carry this gift of knowledge with me forever*
*Always sharing its beauty, splendor, and hope with others*
*Never will I forsake it, never will I deny it, never will I tire*

Summer was a time of long days and warm nights, a time of life at its fullest, a time without school and the stress it brought, both academic and social. Summer was a time when I was really free to be a part of the nature I loved so much. Summer wasn't a time spent only working on the farm; it was a time spent with my friends, swimming in our favorite swimming holes, riding bikes, fishing, and camping, a time of discovering myself and the wonderful place where I grew up.

Fall was a time of harvest, and I loved it. With the exception of wild strawberries and pokeweed, which I cut in the spring for dad to sell at the store, or the maple sap and honey harvest in late winter, everything else was harvested in the fall. The last cut of hay was made and stored, the corn was picked and placed in the corncrib, and the corn stocks were put in shocks in the field. For some reason, I just loved to harvest things, a lot of which weren't part of farming. We had two full-size apple trees. A medium-size red tart grew back by the spring to the north that was great for apple sauce (which Mom made with cinnamon sticks), jelly, and juice. The other, which was also used to make apple sauce, was a very large old-time yellow apple that grew just off the lane to the east. I never knew the names of the apples, but they were very old trees, and I can't remember a year they didn't yield a crop.

We had a lot of fox grapes on the farm, but I never gathered any of them; they were left for the birds and bees. We did have an old Concord grape vine back by the apple tree and spring I just mentioned from which Mom made grape juice and jelly. We had black walnut trees where I gathered nuts that I would then spread on the lane to get run over by cars to get those stain-prone husks off before selling them at the store, as no one much cared for them at home. We did use a lot of nuts from the butternut trees, as we did hickory nuts, but most of the nuts were sold at the store. One thing you don't hear much of anymore is sassafras. I used to dig up the roots of the sassafras trees down by the creek, wash them, and skin the bark off the roots with a knife, then let it dry. Once dry, we sold it at the store in small packages for those who wanted to make sassafras tea.

Old Man Winter usually showed up in late fall with the first forecast of snow, and I would get so excited in anticipation of that event. Those times made such an impression on me that, later on in years, I wrote a poem about it called "It's Almost Ready to Snow," which I would like to share with you.

*       *       *

## *It's Almost Ready To Snow*

*—George Windish, February 2010*

*Damp air is crisp with clouds of gray*
*Temperatures are cold; it's late in the day*
*A circled pale sun dimly rolls on down*
*Very soon bringing darkness all around*

*Stillness haunts the naked woodland deep*
*Winter is coming with its promise to keep*
*White magic will soon fall on a frozen land*
*Surely life has stopped to await its hand*

*No calls from birds in the bushes or trees*
*No rustlings by creatures in the crisp fallen leaves*
*Silence is broken by a distant train whistle*
*Quickly muffled by air as thick as a thistle*

*Feelings are restless with anticipation so high*
*Outside on the porch, eyes gaze up to the sky*
*A faint halo of breath writes wisps barely seen*
*With numbing cold penetrating senses so keen*

*The grandfather clock standing tall and glum*
*Shows the midnight hour has not far to come*
*Oh, one final blind look into the purple dark hue*
*Peaceful sleep is now calling for all flesh to renew*

*Hopeful heart now aflutter, eyes burning with stare*
*Could it be crystalline angles seen floating out there?*
*Coming slowly at first, bringing calmness and light*
*Quickly creating a patchwork of grays in the night*

*The earth now receiving the gift of the season*
*Opens herself up, never questioning its reason*
*The sanctity and beauty that is now to behold*
*Will be seen only through eyes of great stories untold*

Winter is such a beautiful time because it is so different from the other seasons. To start with, it's when Christmas happens, and at the farm, that was a big time. We decorated the house both inside and out. Outside, there were spotlights that lit up the whole house, and those years when we had snow, it looked like a Currier and Ives picture. Inside, Christina decorated all the mantels with greens and crowfeet, and because the old house had tall ceilings, we always had a big Christmas tree that was at least ten feet tall. Mom had plenty of balls and other ornaments to hang on it, and we used to put on the old-fashioned tinsel— the kind that was really heavy and actually made from tin. We had a village under the tree as well as a Lionel freight train with a coal tender, oil car, flatcar, and caboose. I remember when the tinsel would fall on the tracks and short out the train, which always caused a stir.

That Lionel train just fascinated me. When I turned twelve or so, I started building a train platform, which eventually grew to the size of four by twelve feet. It was my masterpiece. All the wiring was under the board, and the tracks were secured to the base as were the telephone poles that lined the track. I used Mom's cotton sewing thread to simulate wires on the poles. All the houses were lit and wired in parallel, so if a bulb went out, I knew which one it was. They were also hand painted and had colored-cellophane windows. I used the two tunnels that came with the Lionel set at each end, and the board itself was painted with dark-green paint, to which I added sand to give it texture.

One Christmas, my grandmother Stacey gave me a new train—a red American Flyer passenger train. It was a real beauty, made up of three lighted Pullman cars, a mail car that picked up and delivered mail, a sleek engine that smoked and whistled, and an equally sleek coal car. That same Christmas, Mom and Dad gave me one of those transformers with two handles, one on each side to control the speed of the trains, as well as two additional knobs to control lights and other accessories. Man, I tell you, I was in tall cotton; I just knew that was by far the best Christmas I ever had!

So, now with two trains, I put the American Flyer on an oval track on the outside of the platform and the Lionel on a figure eight track in the center of the platform. It was just beautiful, and I could sit there on my stool and control the whole thing from my new transformer. You may find this hard to believe, but with the exception of the actual platform and the Lionel set, which my sister Christina has, I still have the whole layout with that fancy transformer. I haven't reconstructed it since before I went to college, but I bet it all still works. I'm going to have to set it up someday soon to see if it still does. That train set was the center of many of my Christmases. I sure was one lucky kid.

*Grandfather Windish, Grandmother Windish, Grandmother Stacey,*
*brother David, Me, Dad and Mother*

Christmas was also an important time for my dad's business, and he would ask me to help by cutting all manner of greens from the farm that could be bundled into sprays and sold at the store. We had quite a few different kinds: white pine, yellow pine, black pine, hemlock, rhododendron, and laurel. I couldn't wait until Dad told me to collect the greens, and long before the time came to cut them, I went out scouting the best locations so I wouldn't waste a minute hunting for them. While gathering, I would use the big farm wagon pulled by the Oliver Row Crop 70 tractor. I had to travel pretty much all over the farm to harvest all the different kinds, as well as the Christmas tree, which was a hemlock.

The hemlocks, which I mentioned in an earlier chapter, grew at the cliff. The young hemlocks were thin and wispy, so I used to climb one of the older ones that was thirty or forty feet or more tall and cut off the top. They were just beautifully shaped, perfect for a Christmas tree. Besides getting the Christmas tree at the cliff, I would cut laurel there as well. The rhododendron was too far down the cliff face for me, so I had to gather it elsewhere, usually along Evitt's Creek below the lower barn. The yellow-and-black pine was taken from along the tree line of the upper forty, and the white pine was gathered on the ridge between the old cabin site and the upper forty. I usually got everything that was needed in one day, always a Saturday, so everyone was home the next day to help bundle it up. The following poem is about cutting the greens.

\* \* \*

# A Christmas Remembered (Cutting The Greens)

—George Windish, 1996

All the hickory nuts had been gathered and the shellbark stood
    tall and naked.
It was late December, and Dad said it was time to cut the greens.
I looked down to the bottomland where yesterday there lay pools
    of rain, now transformed, were great sheets of ice.
The north winds were sharp and cutting and hinted of things
    to come.
I felt good in my heavy wool coat, my warm boots, and my pull-
    down cap.
The cold wind teared my eyes and bit at my cheeks as I looked
    to the west.
The winter fire I saw told me it would soon be supper.
Oh, such a wonderful time to be here, to be home, to be alive.
Tomorrow I would cut the greens and the Christmas tree. How
    could I sleep tonight?
Our Father who art in Heaven, God bless Mom and Dad,
    Grandmom, Grandpop, Chrissie, Gloria, and Dave.
The morning was cold and shivering gray; I hurried to the barn
    still full of warmth and sleep.
That old Oliver tractor, metal green, quiet with frost, objected
    to my plan.
The crank handle was cold, hard to turn, pull the choke, turn
    faster, and watch out for the kick.
The ride was cold and bumpy, trailer in tow up the hill, past the
    now brown clover and timothy fields.

*Through the woods and back to the cliff, a secret place, my place,*
  *shared with only turkeys, deer, and bobcats.*
*The snow began first as only a sound in the great stillness, slowly*
  *building to a natural rhythm on the crisp beech leaves.*
*Quickly, boughs were taken with care, only those which left the*
  *promise of next year.*
*The hemlock with its small cones, the great broom needles of the*
  *yellow pine, the silken leaves of the rhododendron.*
*Saw on my belt, it's a difficult climb, but only the top of the gi-*
  *ant hemlock will do for our    Christmas tree.*
*Twenty, thirty, forty feet. The cut is made, the top falls, and I*
  *stand alone above the forest.*
*The snow is now deep, my heart is full, home is not far, and I*
  *have cut the greens.*

On Sunday afternoon, the whole family would gather in the garage, where a large worktable was set up so the greens could be cut into proper lengths for making sprays. Each spray contained multiple types of green, so when purchased, it could be hung up or used as desired. We had a real assembly line set up, and everyone had a job, so it didn't take too long. Mostly, we made 150–200 sprays. It was an exciting time, with everyone talking and laughing. My grandfather Windish always made wisecracks or told jokes, and my grandmother would tell him to be quiet. Our black cat, Porgy, that my grandfather brought home from the store was always jumping up on the table and had to be shushed off. The dogs were usually quiet in their boxes that fit under the stairwell to the apartment above.

I guess I should explain these boxes. Dad would order fresh fish from a company on the Chesapeake Bay in Christfield, Maryland, which he then sold at Stacey's Market. The fish, packed with ice, were delivered once a week in large wooden boxes that measured about thirty by sixty inches wide and twenty-four inches high and had the lids nailed down—the kind we had to open with a hammer. Dad brought two of the boxes home, and Mom put old coats and linens in them for the dogs to sleep on, which is where they spent most of their time in the winter. The garage was heated, so it was nice and comfortable for the dogs, as well as for us making the sprays. These were great times for all of us, and the customers just loved the fresh greens for their Christmas celebrations.

Another great thing about winter was the cold; it brought the snow and ice. Most winters, the pond froze as well as the creek. Ice meant ice-skating, which everyone enjoyed. Snow meant sledding and tobogganing. When there was a heavy snow, most of the roads would be closed, especially the country roads, so on the way home from school, a group of us kids would plan when and where to meet to go sledding. Many times, we would meet at White's Store up on Bedford Road, and if Bedford Road was closed, we would walk up to the state line, the Mason Dixon Line. Starting at Centenary Church, we would ride down the hill to the beginning of Union Grove Road, and if it was slick enough, we could keep going down Union Grove all the way to the creek. That whole ride was over a mile. Sometimes we would go sledding on a trail in the woods of Smouse's Ridge. Fires would be built, usually in old tires, and once the trail was broken in, we would get the ride of our lives!

The problem with the fires was that, after you passed them, you were temporally blinded. If you weren't in control and didn't know the track, you would crash. One time when I was sledding down the trail, I crashed into a tree after passing a fire and nearly broke my arm. When I lost control, I put up my arm to protect my head. My arm was bleeding pretty badly, so a couple of my friends pulled me home on the sled, which caused quite a stir when I arrived home with the injury. My arm eventually healed, and there wasn't any permanent damage. I still have the scar today on the outside of my left arm.

In later years, we used to ride the toboggan on a hill we called Sugar Loaf, which was located just off Rocky Gap Road and across the creek to the south of the Hasts' place. Tobogganing is probably one of the most thrilling sledding experiences you can have. The only way to control the toboggan is leaning to the left or right to change course, and that must be done in unison with those riding with you. Short of that, the only thing you can do if the toboggan is not going where you want is to jump off. If you want my advice, you should always choose wide-open spaces to go tobogganing.

I have one other story of winter I would like to share with you. We had a long lane leading from the road to the house, and in the winter when we had snowstorms, the lane would drift shut, so it was really difficult for Dad to get to work. It was also a problem if there was an emergency and you had to get out. Well, on March 9, 1947 we had one of those winter storms and an emergency. My mother was pregnant and decided to have my brother David the night of that storm, but of course, Dad couldn't get her to the hospital. Dad called his friend Ed Vandergrift, who owned a construction company. Uncle Ed sent out a piece of heavy equipment to open the lane so Mom could get to the hospital.

After that, Dad decided to buy a snowplow for the Oliver tractor. Well, that was great, but let me tell you a few things about it. First of all, it must have weighed a thousand pounds. It had a solid-steel frame that hooked to the tractor frame with solid-steel pipes and to the back axle with C clamps. The plow was about six feet wide and, of course, was constructed of heavy steel. The blade would only move from side to side, so you had to get off the tractor, pull the pins, and wrestle it to the desired angle. To lift the plow, you had to pull on a huge lever; in my case, it took all the strength I had with all my weight to lift it. But it did the job, and the lane was always open after that, sometimes before the county road.

One winter, after we got a heavy snow, I opened our lane and then decided that I should keep going up the county road to see if anyone else wanted his or her driveway opened for a buck or two, depending on the length of the driveway. My plan was working out just fine. As a matter of fact, when I got to Bedford Road, I kept going toward Cumberland and did a number of driveways there. I went past the fire hall to a small gas station on the right and pulled in to ask the owner if he wanted me to clean out the snow. With his approval, I went back outside and started plowing. I was doing fine until I backed the left tractor wheel into a parked state police car. I was mortified. What to do? I went into the station, found the policeman, and told him what had happened. He went outside, surveyed the damage, and suggested I find another way to earn a living. If I promised not to come up on the state road anymore, he would take care of the dent. Needless to say, I hightailed it home, and that was the last time I went out to plow driveways up on the state highway.

# Chapter 28

# Neighbors

Living where we did was quite remote, and neighbors with children were not close by—close enough to get to with a bicycle, but not next door. I met most of the kids I knew on the school bus. I used to catch the school bus just above the end of our lane at Wentling's garage; it was just an old garage-type building that opened to the road, but it kept us out of the weather when needed. Old Man Wentling, as we called him, wasn't a very nice guy. He didn't like kids, and he didn't like people on his property. He never said anything to me about waiting in the garage to catch the bus, but it made me a little apprehensive. I'll tell you what kind of guy he was; he used to send his dog, a big one, after me when I rode by his house on my bike. It was downhill to my house, so I used to take my feet off the pedals and raise my legs up in the air. That way the dog couldn't latch on to my pant legs and pull me off the bike. I also remember him driving copper nails into our trees that were along his property line to the east to kill them. Ironically, once they died, they fell on his fence line and tore it up. Needless to say, I stayed away from him; there wasn't anything to be learned from him, with the exception of not wanting to be like him. Some people leave rotten legacies.

Back to the bus and the kids I met there. For some reason, there weren't many girls close to my age who rode the bus. One of the two who did was Rosemary Robinson, whom we called Rosie. She was a pretty girl with beautiful long hair who was always really nice to me. Her sister Linda, the youngest of the Robinson children, also rode the bus with us. The girls had two brothers—Nelson, who was the oldest boy, and Steve, who was a year or so older than me. The Robinsons, who lived down by the old schoolhouse on Evitt's Creek, had one other daughter named Margret, or Margie. She was closer in age to my sister Christina, so I didn't know her very well.

When I met Steve, I didn't know much about worldly things. He was an outgoing, smart guy who taught me a lot about hunting and fishing. Steve also introduced me to smoking. Both Steve and Nelson smoked, so I decided that I wanted to smoke too. I must say, though, smoking got me in a lot of trouble when I did it on the school bus. I learned how to spit correctly and to measure who could pee the farthest out from the big bridge down by the swimming hole. I also learned that I had to adorn the handlebars of my bike with squirrel tails that I had shot and to go fast enough downhill so that they would stand out straight in the wind. If they were fox squirrel tails, that was the greatest! As fate would have it, I never shot any fox squirrels, so I had to settle for gray squirrel tails. All those things a boy has to know if he is going to fit in, I learned from Steve.

In the summer, the Robinsons used to build a dam across Evitt's Creek, which flowed behind their house, so they could swim back there, and I got to join them a few times. They were a good family that took care of themselves, always cultivating a big garden and growing everything they needed. The Robinsons also had chickens. Mr. Robinson, whose first name was Nelson, was a very pleasant and nice man whom I often saw working in the garden but never got to know well. Mrs. Robinson, the matriarch of the Robinson family, was a small lady who always treated me well and, on occasion, would give me something to eat. I'm sure I'm correct in remembering that she played the piano, which they kept in their living room. I always admired their family; they lived differently from mine, yet they were really good, hardworking folks, people to learn from, and I did.

There was another boy my age, Bill Gellner, who lived in the next house up from the Robinsons. I'm not sure of the exact spelling of his name, but I do know he didn't have a very good life. I have no idea what happened to his mother, but he lived alone with his father, who raised chickens—I believe for eggs, but I'm not sure. Bill's father always seemed unhappy, and he wasn't good to Bill at all. Bill confided in me that his father would beat him on a regular basis. I always felt sorry for him and tried to be his friend. On occasion, he would come over to the farm, and we always had a good time together. He also hung around with the Robinson boys and came to 4-H, but I never really knew him as a friend. Later in years, I often wondered what happened to people like him. He had a rough start, but he may have turned out fine and made something of himself.

Another boy I really liked was Dave Ferguson, who was a few years older than I. His father had a good-size farm across from the swimming hole, just below the Robinson home on the other side of the road. David was a really nice guy, and for some reason, he really liked me. I remember him as an extremely kind person. He was much bigger than me, and his hands were those of someone who does a lot of hard work—a result of the heavy work he did on his dad's farm, I'm sure. His dad had an old pickup truck—I think it was a Ford—that Dave used to drive over to my house in the summer after finishing his chores. He would ask if I wanted to go to the drive-in movie with him in LaVale. We were usually all sitting around on the front porch, so Mom and Dad always let me go. Dad would give me a dollar, and off we went in that old truck. It was a real treat for me to be able to go out at night without my parents. When we arrived at the drive-in, we would get popcorn and Cokes. Most times, we didn't even know what movie was playing, but that didn't matter; all I knew was it just didn't get any better than that. I really liked being with Dave.

I also remember when Dave's dad put up a basketball hoop in their barn, and in the winter, the neighborhood boys would get together after dinner to play, we picked up teams based on however many guys showed up . I was never too healthy then, as I remember, probably because of the pulmonary problems I had, which were aggravated by the dust in the barn. I used to cough a lot and had trouble breathing, so I wasn't much help to the side I was on, but I liked the game and learned to play it well. It's funny what you remember about people and how you carry that with you throughout your life. Dave is someone I will always have fond memories of. I will remember him as a friend who never questioned me, never expected anything from me, and always treated me with respect; it's hard to say that about many people you meet in your lifetime. Thanks, Dave.

Charlie O'Neal and I were in the same grade, so we had known each other since elementary school. Charlie, or Carty, as we called him, lived on Hazen Road, not too far from my home. I previously mentioned Charlie in the hunting chapter. Charlie's father was the one who sold me the twenty-five-caliber rim fire rifle that didn't have a firing pin. One reason I wanted to mention Charlie is because he, like I, had a connection to Windale. Not when I lived there, but when he was a small boy, he lived with his family in the old tenant house on the farm, so he was a resident of Windale before I was. Another reason I wanted to mention him is that he was and is a solid friend; we spent a lot of time together just doing what boys do. I do remember one time when we kind of got in trouble. Back when we were about fourteen or so, the City of Cumberland contracted to have a new waterline installed, bringing water to the city from the two manmade lakes in Pennsylvania that were built to create reservoirs of drinking water. They constructed the lakes by damming Evitt's Creek in two places. One was named Lake Gordon and the other Lake Koon. Once the land for the pipeline was cleared, the contractor brought in the pipe and laid it along the right of way. The pipes, as I remember, were made of concrete and about ten feet long with a forty-eight-inch diameter. They were almost big enough to stand up in. Carty and I used to play in and on the pipes, which was a lot of fun. One day, we decided to smoke some cigarettes while inside one of the pipes. To make a long story short, his father caught us smoking. I guess it was a calm day and the smoke from our cigarettes was coming out one end of the pipe and then traveling upward, so to anyone nearby, it was obvious what we were doing.

Charlie still lives on Hazen Road, not far from the home where he grew up. Charlie is a jack-of-all-trades who has the skills to do anything, and for the last twenty-some years, he has been building a beautiful new home on the old John Wentling property, just south of Windale. This home is a history museum of materials that he has gathered from all over Allegany County and beyond, which have been tastefully blended together to create an extremely beautiful and well-constructed home. Charlie is an exceptional storyteller, and each acquisition has a marvelous adventure story as to how it was attained. Charlie's voice has never changed; he sounds the same today as he did when we were young boys. His higher, younger voice and total recollection of detail along with the excitement he puts in each story demands your undivided attention. I have tried to encourage him to put his stories in writing so they can be shared with others, but as of this writing, my efforts have been to no avail. I would be remiss if I didn't mention that he has a wealth of knowledge of the surrounding area; he is the man to ask if you need to know anything about its history. Charlie, like other friends I had while growing up at Windale, made an indelible mark on my life and added greatly to the adventures of my youth.

Another story I must tell you before I leave my friends concerns a friend of mine named Eugene Cave, who did not live in my neighborhood, but in town. I met him at Gephart Elementary School in 1945 and we still keep in contact today. Gene married Sondra Weltman who sat in front of me in many of my classes in high school. Gene went to a different high school than I, but because he married Sondra he attends all of my class reunions, so we have kept in close contact since elementary school. Gene and I became very good friends, to the point that we used to stay overnight at each other's house on weekends. I guess we were about ten years old when we started doing it. It was good for both of us. Gene lived in town and didn't know much about the country, and I lived in the country and didn't know much about living in town, so the things we did were quite different from what we were used to. If I stayed at his house, I would walk home with him after school on Friday, and on Saturday, I would walk down Frederick Street to Center Street and one block left to Stacey's Market. I could then come home with Dad after work. Gene, on the other hand, would ride the bus home with me on Friday, which he never had to do to get to school, and then my mom would take him home at the end of the day on Saturday.

I loved to stay at Gene's; he had a monkey in the basement we could play with. I had never seen a live monkey, and it was just a fascinating experience. Staying over at Gene's house was also the first time that I was not with someone from my family overnight. Another whole new experience for me, being a country boy, was walking through the city to the Stacey's.

Thinking back, there were other bicycle-reachable friends who came into my life over the years: Ronnie Layman, Lee Brotemarkel, and maybe others I can't remember anymore who lived in the neighborhood and were a part of my adolescence. However, there are two more of my friends I would like to tell you about, but I'm going to write about them in the following chapters.

# Chapter 29

# Camping Trip

Norney Gilliam, whom I've talked about before, wasn't just a friend he was a co-worker on the farm. As I said before, he lived up on Bedford Road with his parents and his brother Harold. Norney was a year or so older than I, and Harold was about my age or younger. I'm sure I mentioned Norney elsewhere in other chapters when I was discussing fence building, making hay, trapping muskrats, and above all, killing the rats in the chicken coop! Norney was smart and skilled at whatever he did. He used to hunt on the farm with a bow and arrow and usually got his deer. He and I both had an interest in building train sets and hunting, so we always had a lot to talk about. Norney had a great imagination and was always coming up with ideas and stories. One time in particular when we were talking about how Indians had lived in our area, Rocky Gap came up as a place where they used to settle.

Before we go any further with this story, let me tell you about Rocky Gap. Evitt's Mountain, east of our farm, is split by a deep and steep gap near its southern end. I've never heard of the geological reason for the gap's existence, but because of its depth and rocky terrain, it is remotely located and difficult to enter. The only way to access it is from the east or west end of the gap, and upon entering, you have to walk along and sometimes in Rocky Gap Creek to get up into it.

Well, back to the Indians. I'm not sure that they ever did live there, but it sounded right to Norney and me, so we hatched a plan to explore it. There was a lot of discussion about the caves that were said to be there in addition to the bobcats that lived there, along with numerous other animals. There were native trout in the stream, and the water was clean and clear, so Norney, Harold, and I arranged to go camping there for a week. We weren't sure what equipment we would need, because none of us had ever been up there before. We knew we had to travel as light as possible due to it being so hard to get into the gap. Each of us carried a knife and changes of clothes, and together, we took a tent and something to sleep on, rope, and a .22 rifle. We packed pots and pans to cook in and something to carry water in for drinking, as well as forks and spoons, a hammer and nails, and a hatchet. We decided what food we would need, and I got it at Dad's store, all of it being dry and canned goods. The more we prepared, the more excited we became. I thought I would just burst with anticipation in waiting for that day to come.

We readied our packs the night before, so the next morning, we would only have to ride our bikes up Rocky Gap Road about two miles to the west opening of the gap. We hid the bikes in the woods and began the walk in. It was quite a difficult trek, with lots of large boulders and water to navigate, but it was one of the most magnificent places I had ever seen, and it was just a few miles from my house. About halfway in, we started looking for a place to set up camp. We quickly found out why it was called Rocky Gap—nothing but rocks and boulders. There were a lot of trees, big trees, trees so big they were like nothing I had ever seen before. Most of the trees were huge hemlock trees, probably old growth, because no one could harvest them from the gap. The scent in the air was like nothing I had ever smelled before, a scent that forever more would be etched in my memory; when I think about it, I can still smell it today.

Finally, we found a twenty-by-twenty flat area about ten feet above the stream. It was obvious that someone else had been there before us and set up a camp area. There was a place for a campfire and some nails in the trees as well as a small path down to the creek. It was a great place, and we went about the chore of setting up camp. That afternoon, we blocked part of the stream so we would have a pool of water along one side to fetch water from. That first night was not what we'd expected at all. After building a fire, we had something to eat, and then we just sat around the fire and talked until it was time to get some rest. We got situated in the tent and went to sleep quickly, as it had been an exhausting day.

We hadn't been asleep too long before I felt, as did Norney and Harold, that there was something else in the tent with us. Whatever it was, it wasn't that big, but there was more than one. To say the least, there was a mad dash to get out of the tent and find a light to see what was going on. Rats, many wood rats, were all over the place. They didn't seem to be afraid of us, but did scramble when chased. We built the fire back up, but we didn't get much sleep that night, as one of us had to stay awake to guard against the rats coming into the tent. The next morning, we realized the problem—the rats had gotten into some of our food. When rats find food, they put out the alarm to all the other rats to come and get it; well, it seemed like that anyway!

We had to solve this problem—and quick—or one of two things was bound to happen: we would starve to death or die of sleep deprivation. What a mess! All we needed was for it to rain the rest of the time we were there. Anyway, we decided that our food had to be protected, but we had no means to enclose it. We thought of burying it, but the rats would probably dig it up. We could let them have everything but the canned goods, but that would force us to go home early. Finally, we decided to hang the food, except canned goods, from a large tree limb of one of those huge hemlocks with wire hooked to the rope we had brought; that way we could raise and lower it as needed. The rats could get to the rope, but they couldn't get to the food due to the wire. I didn't see any rats try to get to the food, and there was no evidence that they ever did. Once the food was out of the rats' reach, the rat problem ended. We would see one rat once in a while, but no more in the tent.

During the day, we would take food and our knives and the .22 rifle to explore the gap. One day, we climbed the south slope of the gap looking for the Indian caves that were supposed to be there, which we finally found almost at the top. They were small and more like fissures in the rock than caves made by water; nonetheless, they were caves. The view from the top of the gap on the south side is just spectacular; there is an outcrop point just above the caves that you can stand out on and see the whole gap. Looking to the west, you can see all the way across Evitt's Valley to Will's Mountain; looking to the east, you can see all the way to Martin's Mountain. A view that is just as beautiful today as it was back then. Today the creek that runs through the gap is dammed up at the east end of the gap and forms a beautiful lake in Pleasant Valley, the area known as Rocky Gap State Park. The gap itself has not changed much from what it was when Norney, Harold, and I camped there all those many years ago.

One evening, we were sitting around the campfire when we heard something moving north of our camp. It didn't sound too big, but big enough to get our attention; we were still a little shell-shocked after the rat incident. Anyway, the noise stopped, and we forgot about it and turned in for the night. None of us had been asleep long when we heard this terrible cry from an animal—the kind that makes the hair on the back of your neck stand up and you sit right up no matter where you are and listen, which is precisely what we all did. Again, we got out the lights but found nothing. Then, there it was again, the same sound. Only, this time the cry lasted longer than the first, and we had a chance to determine the direction it had come from. It sounded like a baby crying, but loud and long and really scary. All of our lights went to the sound, and about thirty yards from us was a bobcat sitting on a large boulder looking at us. My heart stopped, as I'm sure did that of the other guys. We looked at each other and decided that the best thing to do was to rekindle the fire to see if the cat would go away, and as far as I know, it did. We never heard it again, but you can bet we listened real hard each night thereafter until we left the gap.

The rest of our time there was uneventful. We spent our days exploring or swimming in the gap—which, by the way, was quite cold since it was basically spring fed—and lounging around the camp until it was finally time to leave. The walk out was easier; we had less to carry and knew the way. What an adventure I had with my friends, what a time to remember, how fortunate I was to have had friends like Norney and Harold who enabled me to have those experiences and the memories I now carry with me. A couple of years ago, I talked to Norney's older brother, and he told me Norney now lives in Morgantown, West Virginia. I hope he gets a chance to read this someday.

# Chapter 30

# Road Trip

Robert Wardlow Huck III became my best and closest friend I ever had while growing up. I came to befriend Bob, as I called him, because our fathers knew each other. Bob's mom and dad moved into a home just up Union Grove Road, about halfway up toward Bedford Road, when I was around fourteen years old. Bob's dad asked my dad, since Bob didn't know anyone in the surrounding area, if he would get Bob and me together—which he did.

That's how Bob came into my life, and we became instant friends and have remained so to this day. We were in the same grade level in school, both the same age, and it was a time when we were both just beginning to realize that our lives were changing and we were beginning to come into our own. Bob and I could talk about anything and always had a clear understanding of what the other was thinking. We trusted each other, and that trust was never broken. I tell you this from the bottom of my heart that Bob is the only friend I have ever had in these seventy-three years that has never hurt me in any way. There were never any doubts in our minds about each other. We both loved adventure; neither of us was afraid to take chances. We both had great imaginations and dreams about the future and what our lives held for us. We were good for each other at a time in our lives when there were many temptations. We would talk about those temptations together and, in most cases, made the right decisions about them. Bob is the only man who knows things about my young life that I have never told anyone else. Bob became a part of my family, as I did his. We only had about four years together until our lives were separated; I went to college at Frostburg State Teachers College, and Bob went to Penn State. Bob is an honest man, a man of integrity, a man who is not afraid to show his heart, and I trust him without question. We have kept in contact over the years, and I know a great deal about his life since college which has been very exciting to say the least and would suggest that you read his latest book titled "Alaska Letters", if you would like a copy of it you can email him at Pharquar_99@yahoo.com.

Despite our short time together, there are a few stories from those four years that I would like to share with you. Before I begin, I need to tell you that we spent as much time together as we could, and most of our time together was not the stuff of great stories; it was time shared thinking and doing the simple things we both loved. We traveled through the woods, went hunting, sat on the edge of the pond, and tried to shoot bats (which we never hit, by the way). We went to the movies on Saturday nights, first on the bus to downtown and then later to the drive-in. We talked about things we couldn't talk to anyone else about—and, yes, we talked about girls—trying to understand our feelings as well as trying to understand what all these changes we were going through were all about. We shared those adventures we had with girls and tried to learn from each other. But let me get back to the real stories I want to share with you.

If you remember, I said earlier that, most times, Bob and I made the right decisions when it came to temptations. Well, sometimes we didn't. I remember one time in particular when we were out in the woods with our rifles as usual, and as I recall, it was over near Rocky Gap. We were following a logging trail and came upon a construction trailer parked in the woods. I have no idea why it was there, but there it was. To say the least, we were curious, and the situation was tempting in the following sense: I wonder what is in the trailer? I wonder if the door is unlocked? Should we try to get in?

Well, we couldn't get in the trailer, as it was locked up, so we didn't know what was inside. Since we couldn't get in, we decided it was a good idea to shoot at the trailer—many times. To make a long and stupid story short, the owner caught us in the act. The first question he asked us was, "Do you know what's in the trailer?" To which we replied, "No." So he said, "Let me show you." Would you believe he had dynamite stored in it? If one of us had hit the dynamite with our shots, our lives would have been changed forever, if there were any life left. As it was, we were both still in big trouble. The man who owned the trailer told us that he would not press charges or tell our parents if we repaired the trailer and promised to never do such a foolish thing again. To which we both agreed, and I have never broken that promise.

I must say that we did do a couple of things that were kind of dumb and just a little foolish, as I recall. One time, we dropped a cherry bomb down the chimney of Bob's house and blew ashes all over the living room floor. Lucky for us, there wasn't anyone home at the time, so we were able to clean it up and not get in trouble. Another time, we shot a flaming arrow—actually, a sparkler tied to an arrow—from Bob's crossbow while sitting up on the roof of his house, hitting the neighbor's field and setting it on fire. But I guess, outside of these things, we pretty much stayed true to our word to the man who owned the trailer and gave us a second chance.

I would never say that what we did was excusable due to our youth, but given the temptations that are presented to young boys, Bob and I had pretty good marks. We always played it straight when we took the bus into town on Saturday nights; yes, we shot pool, and there were some strange characters in the pool hall, but we never got involved. There were a lot of paths we could have traveled, but for the most part, we did the right thing. A lot of that came from the fact that our parents trusted us, and we wanted to maintain that trust. I remember one time, though, that my trust in my parents came into question. Bob and I used to catch the ten o'clock bus from town to White's Store on Saturday nights, and one of our parents would pick us up from there. Well, on this particular night, no one showed up, so we decided to walk home. Once we reached Bob's house, I decided to walk the rest of the way alone. It was very dark, but if I looked up at the stars and kept moving, it wasn't too bad. I made it to the creek all right and crossed the bridge, then started walking across the stretch of field from the bridge to the house when all of a sudden a cow—which I didn't know was right there beside me in the pasture—sneezed! Well, I guess I thought it was the end. My heart must have stopped, because my legs gave out, and I went down right there in the middle of the road. I don't think I have ever been so frightened in all my life. I finely got myself together and continued on to the house. When I got there, Mom and Dad had company and were playing cards. They had had a few drinks and forgotten to come get me. But I would say that all parents are entitled to a few mistakes.

When my dad was a young man in his late twenties, he and another man took a cross-country trip from New Jersey to California. I remember hearing him talk about it on occasion, and I saw some pictures that they had taken along the way. Dad was born in 1902, so I'm sure he took the trip before the Depression, probably in the late 1920s. I'm not sure I ever heard why he took the trip, but I know my grandfather Windish had a brother, Bill Windish, who left home on a motorcycle as a young man. He went to California, and nobody ever heard from him again. Dad may have wanted to find out if he had any cousins out there, but he never said whether that was the reason he took the trip. I do know that he did find a cousin, also by the name of Bill, but I never learned where he lived.

I was always intrigued with the idea of doing the same thing someday. One Sunday afternoon during the winter when Bob and I were both sixteen, we were out in the garage at Windale fooling around with the motor on my dad's car, and I told Bob about what Dad had done and how I would like to do the same thing. Bob thought it was a great idea, and from that day on, we started planning our own trip. Both our parents were in agreement to let us go, so we set June 1957 as the target date to leave. The plan was to leave after graduation and after my birthday, which was on June 6, so I would be eighteen and able to get a Social Security card before leaving. As you would expect, we spent many hours planning the route, including what and whom we wanted to see along the way as well as how much cash we would need and how to come up with a car for the trip. Bob's mom and dad solved that problem by buying Bob a car when he was a senior in high school. It was a DKW made by Auto Union in Germany. It had a three-cylinder engine and got about forty miles to the gallon, which was a lot for that time. It was a two-door coupe and quite small, but it had a backseat, so there was plenty of room in the car for the two of us and our stuff.

Neither Bob nor I had traveled much, so it was really exciting when we got on the road. The first day of the trip, we drove through West

Virginia and Virginia until we reached Roanoke, where we stopped for the night. Next, we drove through the Carolinas and Georgia. The following day took us through Florida's west coast to a place called Placida so we could catch a ferry to Gasparilla Island, where we were to meet Bob's uncle Don. He had not arrived yet, so we found his boat and had to cut the lock to get in it so we would have a place to sleep for the night. The only trouble was a hurricane off the coast over near Alabama had the water and weather really stirred up, which made it very difficult to sleep on the boat. The storm had also made the ferry trip a rough one, causing the car's engine to get wet. We couldn't get it started and had to get a push. The next day, we got a message that Don had made arrangements for us to stay in a hotel. The rest of the time there, we did a lot of fishing and each caught big tarpon. Don, a pilot, had flown to Florida and took us up in his small plane. It was my first time ever flying, and what a great time it was. When we left Don, our trip took us through New Orleans; Austin, Texas; New Mexico, where we visited Carlsbad Caverns; and Arizona, where we visited the Grand Canyon, the Painted Desert, and the Petrified Forest along with many other wonderful sights. We then drove to Los Angles and all over California.

Following in my father's footsteps, I decided to see if I too could find some relatives I had never met before. In Downieville, California, I found a second cousin, again named Bill, who lived in an old mill house and was a prospector. Bill took Bob and me to pan for gold, which was something I had never expected. I also found out that Bill had a daughter who lived in North Carolina, but I have never looked for her. After California, we headed for home and saw many sights on our journey, including the Great Salt Lake and the Mormon temple, Yellowstone Park and Old Faithful, Mount Rushmore, and the Badlands in South Dakota. Then we were off to Chicago, where we stayed with Bob's aunt before driving the rest of the way home.

All in all, we were on the road for a month and traveled almost six thousand miles. I kept a diary of the trip, and I can tell you there were many more details that I haven't mentioned, but that may be the stuff of another book, a short story Bob and I could write together. Bob and I had the time of our life, and we still talk about that trip. It cemented an unbreakable bond between us, forever living in our hearts and minds. We are as brothers having shared a slice of our lives together in the years of our youth. We did something that, back then, most eighteen-year-olds never had the opportunity to experience, and it all came about because of the adventuresome spirit of my father, who had planted his seeds in my mind.

# Chapter 31

# Stacey's Market

Cumberland was a railroad town. Both the Baltimore and Ohio Railroad and the Western Maryland Railroad terminals were located there. Their tracks ran right through the city. To get to the store, I had to cross the railroad tracks, of which there were six or eight sets. It was a very large crossing. I had my orders of what to do, but when I got there, it was kind of scary. There was always lot of a train activity, so the railroads had crossing attendants who stopped people and traffic from crossing when a train was moving through. In order to stop people and traffic during the day, they would hold up a big stop sign on a pole, and after dark, they used red lanterns that they would swing back and forth. There was a busy street running parallel to the tracks that I had to cross in order to reach a small waiting area just before the tracks.

One day, just after I had crossed the street, the attendant came out of his little house and held up the stop sign to halt the traffic and me. I looked to my left and saw a very large steam engine pulling a very large train up the tracks. Back then, there were no electric or diesel engines, only coal-burning locomotives. When they first start, they really put out the smoke and are very loud. I was very anxious, to say the least, especially so when I realized the train was coming on the outside track right next to where I was standing. Before the locomotive got to me, I looked over to the attendant, who was looking right at me, and I knew, with that stare, he was telling me to stay put and not to move. Before I had time to think about what was happening, the engine roared past me. It seemed the engine's wheels were as tall as me, with the steam billowing out from behind them and the whistle blowing to warn everyone the train was at the crossing. The ground was shaking, and when I looked down at the tracks, they were moving up and down as each car passed. There was enough wind created by the train that I thought I was going to be blown into the street, also there was thick smoke with a foul sulfur smell everywhere. I felt so small next to that giant steel locomotive; luckily, there was a railing—which I had a steel grip on—between the train and me. After what seemed like a long time, many coal cars and the caboose went by, with a conductor standing out back, and just like that, the train was gone. Brushing soot from my clothes, I looked up to see the attendant waving me across the tracks; he kind of chuckled as I walked by him.

North Center Street in downtown Cumberland, Maryland, was at one time where most of the grocery stores were located. My father opened his store there, on the corner of Center and Henry Streets—51 North Center Street, to be exact. As I mentioned in chapter two, Dad was already working in the grocery business for the American Stores as a sales representative in Johnstown, Pennsylvania, which brought him to Cumberland on business quite often. Liking the area and being a businessman at heart, he decided to start his own business in Cumberland in 1939.

Stacey's was, whenever possible, an open-air market. It had four folding eight-by-four-foot doors made of pane glass that could be opened to the sidewalk in the front of the store, where fresh produce was displayed, especially that which was in season. Fresh strawberries were kept in quart boxes, then wrapped in butcher paper and tied with produce string when sold so they could be carried without damage, as were all other fresh berries we sold, such as raspberries or blueberries. It was an art, but I'll bet I could still do it today; it is kind of like remembering how to tie your shoes. I remember big piles of fresh corn on display tables as well as asparagus, peaches, pears, apples, and all kinds of great food.

Besides having the standard dry goods of most stores, Stacey's specialized in fresh produce as well as fresh seafood brought in from the Chesapeake Bay. Cumberland had a large population of Catholics, and back then, most people ate fish on Fridays, as the Church directed. The seafood was the centerpiece of the business, with the locally grown produce following close behind. The seafood had to be flown in or trucked in from Crisfield, Maryland. Shrimp was supplied in frozen five-pound boxes from the Gulf Coast. There was always a great variety of fish in the seafood case, such as flounder, sea bass, porgies, whiting, rock bass, and butterfish, and on a seasonal basis, there was sea trout, mackerel, and shad. We always had three grades of fresh Chincoteague oysters from Virginia: standard, large, and counts that could be purchased in half-pint, pint, or quart containers. Also, the market always had fresh blue claw crabmeat—in cans with tops you could see through—which also came in three grades: claw, regular, and back fin. When in season, we used to get live soft-shell crabs that came in wooden boxes, packed in seaweed with four dozen crabs per box. There was always fresh-cooked shrimp, seasoned in Old Bay, which Dad prepared in the back room on an old gas stove. When he cooked them, you could smell that wonderful aroma all over Center Street. Dad always had salt mackerel and herring in wooded tubs as well as dried herring for sale. I may have missed some specialty items, but that is primarily what was offered. All these items were displayed on ice in the seafood case during shopping hours and covered with ice at night. Each morning, the ice company on Frederick Street delivered the crushed ice by the bushel in canvas containers.

At the end of every Saturday, all the unsold fish from the week's business, if possible, were cut into fillets and frozen, later to be sold on sale or when not in season. Everything else that could be kept over was packed in ice and stored in the big walk-in cooler in the back room until the following Monday. Some fish had to be thrown out, but that was seldom. Dad was extremely good at his ordering; he kept records of his weekly orders and used them as a guide the next year. He even specifically ordered his seafood from home on Tuesday morning before going to work so it would arrive on Wednesday. There was only a partial display of seafood on Monday and Tuesday, but on Wednesday, the case was full again.

During the growing season, Stacey's sold a great variety of produce from local farmers. Dad always tried to have the best and be the first to have it. The season usually started out with the berries—strawberries, then red and black raspberries—which were all sold by the quart in wooden boxes, followed by asparagus, rhubarb, and green peas, which, for the most part, came from the Miltenberger farm in West Virginia.

There was always a rush to have the first corn and tomatoes. A farmer in West Virginia by the name of Stump often had fresh corn on the cob just before the Fourth of July, and he always came around to Stacey's with his first picking. It was expensive, but we always sold out, so it wasn't a problem. Shortly thereafter, the other farmers had corn, and the price came down. Tomatoes were a different story. Local tomatoes came quite a bit later, but there was a farmer in Garrett County, Maryland, who raised hothouse tomatoes, the beefsteak type. He would bring them into the store early in the season, long before anyone else had them, in small wooden-handle baskets, which we would set on the counter by the cash register, and it didn't take long until they were gone. Back then, tomatoes were only available locally, for the most part, and to have them available so soon before the regulars came in was a real treat.

Dad also had green beans, lima beans, shell beans, turnips, and radishes, even pokeweed and just about anything else you could think of in the vegetable line. He knew his produce, and customers always knew they would get good quality and a fair price at Stacey's. Later in the season came the blueberries, peaches, apricots, plums, pears, and then apples of many varieties, starting with the early applesauce type, then the later Red and Golden Delicious for eating, and finally, the baking types of Wine Sap and Rome Beauty. We also sold pumpkins, rutabagas, local potatoes, and even horseradish root and hickory nuts. If there were a market for it, Stacey's would have it.

From the time I was about thirteen, I started working at the market. At first, it was during busy times like Christmas or the Fourth of July or Easter, but eventually, I began working regularly, except when I was at school or working on the farm. Before I learned to drive, Mother used to take me to town on occasion when she had to accompany me, like if I needed shoes or to visit Dr. Brings for an appointment, but other than that, except for going to school, I stayed on the farm. Going to town back then was an event. Dad insisted that we were dressed up in our best clothes and good shoes, and we had to stop in at the store to say hello. There, he would give us the once-over before we were allowed to go down to Baltimore Street, where the department stores were. Everyone dressed to go to town back then in Cumberland, and I'm sure he didn't want us to be any different just because we lived in the country.

Once I learned to drive and got my license, I would go to the store in the morning with Dad and help set up before I went to school. I would then take the car to school and drive back to the store after school to finish the day and help close up for the night. All the merchants in downtown Cumberland were closed on Sundays, but they all stayed open until nine o'clock on Monday nights, so I also had to work then. I didn't have a lot of free time, but I didn't mind. The only problem was I never got to play sports in high school. Both Coach Cavanaugh, who coached basketball, and Coach Hawn, who coached football, asked me to go out for their sports, but it wasn't meant to be. To me, however, working at the store was an exciting experience, one that I would never regret. It was a time for me to realize and understand a whole other world that I hadn't known. It, along with later experiences, set me on a path that has always brought me happiness and success.

As I spent more time at the store and gained experience in working with customers, I was given more and more responsibility. Dad always told me that I was just as good as anyone else, and regardless of who they were, I should act accordingly around them. He always told me to respect all customers and treat them fairly, but there were rules that the store expected them to abide by. A good example was when we got bing cherries form Washington State. They came in wooden boxes, the top layer of which had all the cherries in perfect rows with no stems showing. The ones on top weren't any better than what was below; however, having them that way made for a good display to sell them. I remember there were times when some customers would get a bag and start picking entire rows off the top. Dad would ask if he could help and respectfully explained why we couldn't allow anyone to do that. Most people would respect the request, but some wouldn't, so Dad would ask them to leave the store. His philosophy was that Stacey's was better off without some customers. But most of those asked to leave would come back after a short time and shop at the market again. We always had quality goods of all kinds that customers wanted. There was no need for some of them to have special treatment because of who they were or what they wanted to do. This was only one of many actions customers would take that we did not allow at the market. Once I started working full-time, I had to abide by the store rules and ask customers to refrain from those actions, and I never felt uncomfortable in doing so, even when they would go to Dad and complain, because he always supported me.

Dad always insisted that everything we sold had to be displayed properly. Everything had had a place, and everything had to be in its place. Everything was presented with quality and order. It was my job to see that displays were always full and in order. It didn't take me too long to figure out how Dad wanted things displayed, so when I wasn't busy with a customer, I was keeping the displays current and in order. I must have learned my lesson well, because even today, I must keep things in order and in their place, to the point that it must be difficult for those around me. I'm sure if you asked my daughter or wife, they would be glad to explain it. Another thing Dad insisted on was starting the day with a freshly starched apron; all the employees had to wear one. Dad, on the other hand, never wore one, which always confused me. Instead, he wore a white shirt and tie; I guess he wanted everyone to know he was the boss. As an aside, most people knew he was the boss but didn't know him as Mr. Windish. Everyone called him Mr. Stacey, and he never corrected anyone—that I know of.

It wasn't too long before I was told to learn the seafood business and had to start spending as much of my time as possible behind the fish case. I loved working there for two reasons, the first of which was already knowing a lot about fish from the time I spent with Grandmother Stacey at the beach in New Jersey, but the second was the most important! That's where Grandfather Windish worked, and I just loved being around him because he was so much fun. He was a lot different than my dad, and I felt a lot less stress. He taught me everything he knew about what I needed to know to work there: how to use the scale, how to clean and fillet fish, how to wrap them, and of course, how to make customers laugh and enjoy their visit. He knew everybody and made sure I did too. Everyone found out quickly that I was his grandson. He told everyone stories about all the dumb things I had done on the farm or at the store, but he told good stories too about what a hard worker I was. He was a natural-born storyteller and jokester. I heard some of the jokes he told so many times I will never forget them and even tell some of them today. When asked what we raised on the farm, he always responded by saying, "We raise hell and weeds." He was in his late seventies and as sharp as a tack; he never missed a trick or a day's work.

Sometimes I used to complain to him about the way Dad was treating me, and he would say, "Don't pay any attention to him; he wasn't too smart when he was your age, either." I was never too sure how to take that. He loved the fresh Chincoteague oysters we sold and would slurp one down and say to me, "You've got to try one," so one day I did and never looked back. I have been eating raw oysters ever since. Sometimes when I was passing by the seafood counter to the back room, he would slip me a peeled cooked shrimp to eat or a piece of dried salt herring.

Stacey's had fresh bread delivered daily from an Italian bakery. They used to deliver large loaves of bread in paper sacks—the kind that was open at one end. The bread was always oven warm, which made the whole store smell of fresh baked bread. I remember one morning when Pop told me to sneak down to the bread rack, get one of the fresh loaves, and bring it to the back room. So I waited until the time was right—couldn't let dad see me do it. I grabbed one loaf and took it to the back room. Pop and I cut it up with a fish knife, spread it with fresh butter from the farm, and ate the whole thing! Sometimes you never forget and that certainly was one of them.

Working with and around Pop were some of the best times of my life. You know, when I think about it, I never saw him angry, I never heard him raise his voice, and I never heard him say an unkind word about anyone. Pop always kept me on balance with my father and was a great refuge from my dad during stormy times. I learned one thing from my grandfather that my dad was unable to teach me: how to openly love my children. I understood my grandfather much more than I ever understood my father, which was difficult for me to comprehend. After all, my grandfather raised my father!

Before I leave Stacey's Market, I want to tell you about some special times I had working there. To me, the two best and most exciting times to work at the store were Christmas and Easter. I'm not sure I could choose which was best, so I'll start with the Christmas season. Being in the food business at Christmastime, you make every effort to have those certain items folks want that are special to them, and Stacey's did just that. We had products in the store at those times that we never carried during any other period of the year. For example, we would have bulk nuts of all kinds by the barrel: Brazilian and English walnuts, filberts, almonds, pecans, hickory, black walnuts, and butternuts. We also had all kinds of citrus: tangerines, navel oranges, kumquats, lemons, limes, tangelos, Florida oranges (for juice), and grapefruit. Dad always ordered mistletoe from some place in Louisiana; we cut and tied it up into sprigs using red ribbon and displayed them on white paper in a special place. We had small cedar Christmas trees that came a dozen to a box; they were about two feet tall, some green, some silver, some white. They stood on folding wooden stands and were displayed all over the store. We had the sprays of greens made on the farm that I spoke of earlier. There were fruitcakes of all sizes and specially baked breads as well as oysters for dressings, sweet potatoes, and plenty of the normal stores we carried to be sure we did not run out during this particular season.

Easter, on the other hand, was an entirely different experience; it started with Lent and ran through Easter Sunday. Seafood was in high demand, and each week, especially Friday, was very busy. During that time, I worked mainly behind the seafood counter, and my job was to scale and clean or fillet the fish. Coming up on Good Friday, the store turned into a madhouse. Shad was the most popular fish, so we took orders for the two weeks before Easter. Some people wanted roe shad with the roe left in, some wanted buck shad, some wanted just the roe shad without the roe, and some wanted just the roe, and all the orders had to be done by a certain day and time. So you can imagine how important it was to get it right the first time; there was no room for mistakes, and my dad made that very clear to me. Remember, all of these fish had to be scaled and cleaned on a schedule. It wasn't like you could do the work ahead of time. We were dealing with fresh fish, and people expected them to be fresh and ready when they came in the store to pick them up.

Dad ordered the shad according to the orders people had placed, plus enough for the pickup customers, and the numbers had to be close, because after Easter, there was very little call for shad. We received many boxes of iced shad on Wednesday morning and placed them in the walk-in cooler, then pulled them as we started filling orders. As I said, it was a madhouse for Pop and me, and sometimes Dad had to help to get the job done on time. As you may expect, there was a lot of tension between Dad and me, but I always survived to live another day.

I enjoyed working during both the Christmas and Easter seasons because of the happiness that I shared with customers and the pleasantries we exchanged. It was good for me as a young man and a good time in my life, from which I took many lessons that have helped me greatly in understanding people later in life.

*Stacey's Market*

# Chapter 32

# Looking Back

Writing this book has given me the opportunity to remember in detail the formative years of my life and to relive in my mind all those wonderful experiences that I was fortunate enough to have. It has also given me a chance to examine the wisdom of my understandings and the value of conclusions drawn.

As you can tell from this book, my father had a tremendous impact on my thinking as I wrestled with youth. He provided wealth, security, a family, a comfortable home, and a life that was full of opportunity and beauty. The one most important part of my life's puzzle that he did not provide was an outward love for me and to assure me that I had value. I longed for that so much that it consumed much of my thoughts. During my time with him, I did all I could to draw out that which I needed from him.

Yet, it was to no avail, which is still difficult for me to grasp. I knew so little of him from verbal communication that I would turn to my senses to try to understand. I used to stand close to him so I could smell him and touch him, as if it were by mistake to know how he felt. I used to relight and smoke cigarettes he had thrown away in my quest. When working at the store and not busy, I used to lean against the fresh produce case while he sat on a stool by the cash register, and when he wasn't looking, I would study his every feature. Above all, I listened without fail to everything I heard him speak. I never kissed my father, but the day I was leaving for the Philippines as part of the Army Security Agency for two years, I did hug him then. I am so thankful that happened, because I never saw him again, as he died two months after I left.

When in the Philippines, I wrote him letters and expressed my feelings and sorrows about how I wished our relationship could have been closer and more open and that maybe we could do something about it after I got home. I never received any reply, so he was true to his character to the very end. I had just gotten married before I left, and being the optimist I am, I just knew that if I was successful and raised a good family, he would finally come around to me. But alas, that too was also lost.

I have always loved him, however; I feel I do not have the knowledge or wisdom to judge him. I have taken all that he taught me, both good and bad, to form my life to give it value.

I hope this book will bring value to your life and provide a snapshot of the life of a young boy in the 1940s and 1950s. I also hope that it may shine the light of understanding on the difficulties of youth brought on by the egos, fears, and misunderstandings of their parents. It has taken me a lifetime to try to better understand my father, and I continue that search with an opened heart.

\* \* \*

# *Opened Heart*

—George Windish, March 2012

Having always opened my heart to the world
My blood flows freely without question
Looking forever to that which is to come
Sensing I am destined to always be within it

Coming closer now to the mountain crest
Strength is less abundant and willing
Looking back over the chosen path to run
The light of past awareness rolls hazily

Encounters of life are studied more slowly now
Studied without fear of consequence or dread
Old skin of youth promptly shed, morph complete
The wisdom of ages becomes ours to behold

Conclusions once drawn now come into question
Measuring their weight a burden heavy to bear
Hot tears flow freely with despair, anguish, and pain
Now grasping the true chronicle of life with its flaws

There is no perfect person, time, place, or event
With contempt comes truth for the soul to witness
Wherein lies the troika of disappointment, sorrow, and grief
Also, a consciousness that faith, love, and joy are their balance

# My Father's Mansion

*Organizing the clutter of life into orderly fashion*
*Patiently, tight knots of entanglement are undone*
*Its darkness becomes clear to an unfettered eye*
*Comparing not judging brings forth revelation*

*The realization of mortality always a companion of thought*
*Arranging the steps of life still are wrought with confusion*
*But life's blurred colors slowly become a delightful rainbow*
*Wisdom prevails, building an ark of honest perception*

*Now at peace, I await God's call*

# Epilogue

Remembering How the Torch Was Passed

My father was always a mystery to me, a mystery I was destined never to solve. A man of great strength laced with many weaknesses. A man I looked up to, yet feared and hid from. A man who mostly lived in the darkness within him, but could burst forth as the sun from behind a cloud. He abhorred weakness, yet unwillingly succumbed to it in the end. A man unable to accept less than perfect, corrected his own imperfections in his children. I was always dismayed by his objectives, confused by his method, yet still understanding of the result. A great deal of him still lingers in my soul.

* * *

## *Hello, Dad*

—George Windish, June 2003

*Boy, it sure has been a long time since we talked*
*Come to think of it, we never did talk too much*

*Thinking back, when I was real small, I don't remember much*
*about you*
*I guess you were on the road, or running the market, or the road*
*stand*

*I do remember we had a fine house and a nice yard*
*I also remember you and Mom had horses and I had a bike*

*Remember when you bought the old farmhouse on Union Grove*
*Road?*
*I remember the day we moved there—everything was so beauti-*
*ful and exciting*

*As you know, when I was young, I wasn't too strong and I was*
*sick a lot*
*Mom was always there when I was sick, but I don't remember you*

*Don't get me wrong, you provided the best a boy could have in*
*worldly things*
*Hey, I do remember you dropping me off at Gephart Elementary*
*School*

# Epilogue

I remember one winter's day when you actually rode the sled
    down the hill
Mom scolded you for doing that because of your arthritic back
    and all

Boy, it's amazing that I remember that after all these years
I remember you doing paperwork on Sunday afternoons and
    smoking a lot

I'm sure you remember more about me 'cause you talked to Mom
I'm sure Grandmom and Grandpop told you things about me also

I used to try real hard to get you to notice me—remember I used
    to shine your shoes?
And I used to fill the stoker with coal every night and take the
    clinkers out of the furnace

In the winter, I would sit in the dark in the sunroom and watch
    for your car
When you started in the lane, I used to run to the garage and
    open the door

I wasn't a very good student, though, and I remember that upset
    you a lot
I really wish I had had a little more help 'cause I know I could
    have done better

One thing I know that you taught me well was to be an achiever,
    a hard worker
You taught me to get the job done quickly and to do it right the
    first time

*Oh, another thing I learned was if you do a good job, you don't
get in trouble*
*Boy, I learned to pay attention to detail and to think things
through*

*Wow, do you remember when the horse ran away with me on the
dump rake?*
*It turned over, and you were really mad, but the horse and I were
OK—I really couldn't stop her*

*One thing I never told you was when the main drive gear on the
new side delivery rake broke*
*Mom and I drove all the way to Frostburg to get a new one, and
I fixed it by myself*

*All I really wanted to do was to grow up to be like you so I could
earn your respect*
*I remember you smoked a lot, so I wanted to smoke and I did and
you knew it*

*Remember how much I loved hunting and just shooting a gun?*
*I bought that old octagon barrel twenty-five-caliber rim fire
without a firing pin and fixed it up*

*It worked pretty well—except the finishing nail I used for a fir-
ing pin was always falling out*
*When you found out what I was doing from Mom, you secretly
bought me a new shotgun—wow!*

*I remember when you brought it home that night I just couldn't
believe you had done it*

*And the very next day, you went hunting with me even though*
*you didn't like to hunt*

*I remember you didn't laugh too much—you always seemed to*
*be off somewhere thinking*
*You really laughed, though, when that cow pooped on me when*
*we were loading her on the truck*

*I loved that farm—you may not know it, but that's the best*
*thing you ever did for me*
*I am what I am today because of the time I spent there and at*
*the fish market*

*I was so proud when you put me in charge of the hired help dur-*
*ing hay season*
*You even had enough trust in me to let me run the market on*
*Monday nights by myself*

*You never told me, but I knew in my heart that you thought I*
*was all right*
*Mom said that you used to tell other people how proud you were*
*of me*

*You made sure I spoke to the customers politely and was always*
*fair and courteous*
*You taught me that I was as good as anyone, and that's as im-*
*portant as anything*

*I remember when I graduated from high school and it was out-*
*side in the stadium*

*You and Mom were sitting there in the middle, and I didn't see*
*anyone else*

*Thanks for insisting that I go to college, after they said you were*
*wasting your money*
*You know, I think that made me more determined than ever, and*
*I didn't do too bad, either*

*I'll bet you remember that MGA sports car I bought after college*
*You and Mom used to take it for a ride on Sundays, and that*
*made me feel really great*

*You were not too happy when I joined the army—no one in our*
*family had ever been in the service*
*I used to write you letters and send them to the market so they*
*would be just between us*

*I was real proud when you liked Linda, and you even took a day*
*off work to come to the wedding*
*Linda told me later that you said you were proud of me, but you*
*didn't like me going over alone*

*Boy, I remember the day I left for Southeast Asia and I gave you*
*a big hug*
*You know, that was the only time that happened—I've spent a*
*lot of time thinking about that*

*And, Dad, two months later, you died and I felt so sorry that our*
*time was over—it just wasn't fair*
*I was just starting my life on my own, and I wanted to show you*
*all the things I could do*

# Epilogue

*Sometimes, when I think about us, I get angry and sometimes sad,
    but there were good times*
*I think if we could have just gotten closer, we would have been
    good for each other*

*I just wanted to say that I really miss you and love you and
    thank you for all you did for me*
*I know that if you were still here, we would work out our differences*

*Maybe one of these days we will get together and talk about it*
*I really look forward to that*

*Windale, when I left home.*

# Acknowledgements

Thank you Linda, my dear wife, for all the reading and editing you did for me. Thank you for putting up with all the craziness I generated when I was writing. Your constant support was the rock that made all this happen. I could have never made it this far without you.

Thank you to Amy and John Shuman for all your support and help. Also, thank you both for giving me the opportunity to share my poetry with the good people of Cumberland, and thank you John for providing my picture for the back cover of this book. It is always good to make new friends.

Thank you Christina, my sister, the first girl I ever loved. Thank you for all your help, input and the editing you did for me. Your support and encouragement gave me the confidence I needed to finish this book.

Thank you Mary Miltenberger for letting me stay in my old home for many summers, which gave me the opportunity to remember all those wonderful times I had living at Windale. That time gave me the inspiration I needed to write this book and to relive a wonderful time in my life.

Thank you to my editor at CreateSpace for the great job she did in helping a novice like me to publish this book correctly and with pride. It amazed me how well she understood the direction I wanted the book to go and the insight she provided to support it.

Lastly, I want to thank the Key Writers group of Big Pine Key, Florida for their critique of some chapters and poetry of this book. Also, in particular I want to thank poet/writer Jeanne Patric, one of Key Writers members, for reading my proof book and catching all those nasty little errors that all the rest of us had missed as well as giving me her professional support.

Made in the USA
Charleston, SC
24 November 2013